Praise for Ijeoma Oluo and
So You Want to Talk About Race

"I don't think I've ever seen a writer have such an instant, visceral, electric impact on readers. Ijeoma Oluo's intellectual clarity and moral sure-footedness make her the kind of unstoppable force that obliterates the very concept of immovable objects."

—LINDY WEST, *New York Times* bestselling author of *Shrill*

"*So You Want to Talk About Race* strikes the perfect balance of direct and brutally honest without being preachy or, worse, condescending. Regardless of your comfort level, educational background, or experience when it comes to talking about race, Ijeoma has created a wonderful tool to help broach these conversations and help us work toward a better world for people of color from all walks of life."

—FRANCHESCA RAMSEY, host and executive producer of MTV's *Decoded*

"Ijeoma Oluo is armed with words. Her words are daggers that pierce through injustice, while also disarming you with humor and love."

—HARI KONDABOLU, comedian, writer, and co-host of *Politically Re-Active*

"You are not going to find a more user-friendly examination of race in America than Ijeoma Oluo's fantastic new book. The writing is elegantly simple, which is a real feat when tackling such a thorny issue. Think of it as Race for the Willing-to-Listen."

—ANDY RICHTER, writer and actor

"When you need a super team to help you make sense of today's complex conversation on identity and representation, Ijeoma needs to be your number one pick. No one cuts

through the chatter with more humor, insight and clarity. No matter the issue, Ijeoma's thinking is always essential reading."
—JENNY YANG, comedian, writer, and co-founder and co-producer of Dis/orient/ed Comedy

"Oluo has created a brilliant and thought-provoking work. Seamlessly connecting deeply moving personal stories with practical solutions, readers will leave with inspiration and tools to help create personal and societal transformations. A necessary read for any white person seriously committed to better understanding race in the United States."
—MATT MCGORRY, actor, *Orange Is the New Black* and *How to Get Away with Murder*

"A clear and candid contribution to an essential conversation."
—*Kirkus*

"In a time where more folks are willing to fall-in-line with whatever political or social commentary others are engaging with, Ijeoma Oluo has ripped that norm to shreds. . . . While so many people want to become 'thought leaders,' 'bloggers,' or even just 'influential,' Oluo is eons past that. . . . Oluo is out to help put words to action, which at this day and age, might be exactly what we need."
—*Forbes*

"Everyone should be paying attention to Ijeoma Oluo."
—*The Root*

"Ijeoma Oluo has emerged as one of Seattle's strongest voices for social justice. . . . Best of all, she gets her message across with incisive wit, remarkable humor and an appropriate magnitude of rage."
—*Seattle* magazine

So you want to talk about race

Ijeoma Oluo

SEAL PRESS

Seal Press
Hachette Book Group
1290 Avenue of the Americas, New York, NY 10104
sealpress.com
@SealPress

Printed in the United States of America
First Edition: January 2018

Published by Seal Press, an imprint of Perseus Books, LLC, a subsidiary of Hachette Book Group, Inc.The Seal Press name and logo is a trademark of the Hachette Book Group.

The Hachette Speakers Bureau provides a wide range of authors for speaking events. To find out more, go to www.hachettespeakersbureau.com or call (866) 376-6591.

The publisher is not responsible for websites (or their content) that are not owned by the publisher.

Print book interior design by Linda Mark.

Library of Congress Cataloging-in-Publication Data
Names: Oluo, Ijeoma, author.
Title: So you want to talk about race / Ijeoma Oluo.
Description: First edition. | New York, NY: Seal Press, 2018.
Identifiers: LCCN 2017041919 (print) | LCCN 2017043938 (ebook) |
  ISBN 9781580056786 (e-book) | ISBN 9781580056779 (hardback)
  Subjects: LCSH: United States—Race relations. | Intercultural
  communication. | BISAC: SOCIAL SCIENCE / Ethnic Studies / African
  American Studies. | SOCIAL SCIENCE / Black Studies (Global). |
  POLITICAL SCIENCE / Political Freedom & Security / Civil Rights.
  Classification: LCC E184.A1 (ebook) | LCC E184.A1 O454 2018 (print) |
  DDC
  305.800973—dc23
LC record available at https://lccn.loc.gov/2017041919ISBNs: 978-1-
58005-677-9 (hardcover), 978-1-58005-678-6 (e-book)

LSC-C

13

Contents

*[REPLACE w/
GENDER
SEXUAL IDENT
ETC —*

So you want to talk about race

A S A BLACK WOMAN, RACE HAS ALWAYS BEEN A PROM-
inent part of my life. I have never been able to escape
the fact that I am a black woman in a white supremacist country. My blackness is woven into how I dress each morning,
what bars I feel comfortable going to, what music I enjoy,
what neighborhoods I hang out in. The realities of race have
not always been welcome in my life, but they have always been
there. When I was a young child it was the constant questions
of why I was so dark while my mom was so white—was I
adopted? Where did I come from? When I became older it
was the clothes not cut for my shape and the snide comments
about my hair and lips and the teen idols that would never
ever find a girl like me beautiful. Then it was the clerks who
would follow me around stores and the jobs that were hiring
until I walked in the door and then they were not. And it was
the bosses who told me that I was too "loud," the complaints

that my hair was too "ethnic" for the office, and why, even though I was a valued employee, I was making so much less money than other white employees doing the same job. It is the cops I can't make eye contact with, the Ubers that abandon their pickup, driving on instead of stopping when they see me. When I had my sons, it was the assumptions that they were older than they were, and that their roughhousing was too violent. It was the tears they came home with when a classmate had repeated an ignorant comment of their parent's.

But race has also been countless hours spent marveling at our history. Evenings spent dancing and cheering to jazz and rap and R&B. Cookouts with ribs and potato salad and sweet potato pie. It has been hands of women braiding my hair. It has been reading the magic of the words of Toni Morrison, Maya Angelou, and Alice Walker and knowing that they are written for you. It has been parties filled with Jollof rice and fufu and Nigerian women wearing sequin-covered gowns and giant geles on their heads. It has been the nod to the black stranger walking by that says, "I see you fam." It has been pride in Malcolm, Martin, Rosa, and Angela. It has been a room full of the most uninhibited laughter you've ever heard. It has been the touch of my young son as he lays his hand over mine and says "We're the same brown."

Race, my race, has been one of the most defining forces in my life. But it is not something I always talked about, certainly not the way that I do now.

Like many people, most of my days were spent just trying to get by. Life is busy and hard. There are work and kids and chores and friends. We spend a lot of time bouncing from one mini-crisis to the next. Yes, my days were just as full of microaggressions, of the pain and oppression of racism, as they are now—but I just had to keep going on like normal. It is very hard to survive as a woman of color in this world, and I remember saying once that if I stopped to feel, really feel, the pain of the racism I encountered, I would start screaming and I would never ever stop.

So I did what most of us do, I tried to make the best of it. I worked 50 percent harder than my white coworkers, I stayed late every day. I dressed like every day was a job interview. I was overpolite to white people I encountered in public. I bent over backwards to prove that I was not angry, that I was not a threat. I laughed off racist jokes as if I didn't feel the sting. I told myself that it would all be worth it one day, that being a successful black woman was revolution enough.

But as I got older, as the successes I had reached for slowly became a reality, something inside me began to shift. I would try to make my voice quieter in meetings and I couldn't. I would try to laugh off the racist jokes and I couldn't. I would try to accept my boss's reasons for why I could have my promotion but not my raise, and I couldn't. And I started talking.

I started to question, I started to resist, I started to demand. I wanted to know why it was considered a bad thing that I was "opinionated," I wanted to know what exactly it was about my hair that was "unprofessional," I wanted to know what exactly it was about that joke that people found "funny." And once I started talking, I couldn't stop.

I also started writing. I shifted my food blog into a "me" blog, and started saying all the things that everybody around me had always said were "too negative," "too abrasive," and "too confrontational." I started writing down my frustrations and my heartbreak. I started writing about my fears for my community and my family. I had started to see myself, and once you start to see yourself, you cannot pretend anymore.

It did not go over well. My white friends (having grown up in Seattle, the majority of my friends were white), some of whom I'd known since high school, were not happy with the real me. This was not the deal they had struck. Yes, they would rage over global warming and yell about Republican shenanigans, but they would not say a word about the racial oppression and brutality facing people of color in this country. "It is not my place," they'd explain when in frustration I'd beg for some comment, "I don't really feel comfortable." And as I looked around my town and saw that my neighbors were not really my neighbors, as I saw that my friends no longer considered me "fun," I began to yell even louder. Somebody had to hear me. Somebody had to care. I could not be alone.

Like dialysis, the old went out and in came the new. Suddenly, people I had never met were reaching out locally and from all across the country in person and online, just to let me know that they had read my blog post and in reading it, they felt heard. Then online publishers started reaching out to me, asking if they could republish my work. And locally, isolated and invisible people of color started reaching out, showing me that I did have neighbors after all.

I was talking and writing at first for my very survival, not for anybody else's benefit. Thanks to the power and freedom of the Internet, many other people of color have been able to speak their truths as well. We've been able to reach out across cities, states, even countries, to share and reaffirm that yes, what we are experiencing is true. But the Internet has a very wide audience, and even though we were writing for ourselves, the power of the hurt, anger, fear, pride, and love of countless people of color could not go unnoticed by white people—especially those who were genuinely committed to fighting injustice. While some had chosen to turn away, upset that this unpleasantness had invaded their space of cat videos and baby pictures, others drew closer—realizing that they had been missing something very important all along.

These last few years, the rise of voices of color, coupled with the widespread dissemination of video proof of brutality and injustice against people of color, has brought the urgency of racism in America to the forefront of all our consciousness. Race is not something people can choose to ignore anymore. Some of us have been speaking all along, and have not been heard. Others are trying out their voices for the first time.

These are very scary times for a lot of people who are just now realizing that America is not, and has never been, the melting-pot utopia that their parents and teachers told them it was. These are very scary times for those who are just now realizing how justifiably hurt, angry, and terrified so many people of color have been all along. These are very stressful times for people of color who have been fighting and yelling and trying to protect themselves from a world that doesn't care, to suddenly be asked by those who've ignored them for so long, "What has been happening your entire life? Can you educate me?" Now that we're all in the room, how do we start this discussion?

This is not just a gap in experience and viewpoint. The Grand Canyon is a gap. This is a chasm you could drop entire solar systems into. But no matter how daunting, you are here because you want to hear and you want to be heard. You are here because you know that something is very wrong and you want a change. We can find our way to each other. We can find a way to our truths. I have seen it happen. My life is a testament to it. And it all starts with conversation.

There is a good chance that you, regardless of race, have tried to have these conversations in the past. There is also a good chance that they have not gone well. So "not well" that perhaps you have been afraid to ever have these conversations again. If that is you, you are not alone. Part of the reason I decided to write this book is because I regularly hear people of all races saying things like, "How do I talk to my mother in law about the racist jokes she makes?" or "I just got called out for being racist but I don't understand what I did wrong" or "I don't know what intersectionality is and I'm afraid to say so." People find me on online messaging platforms and beg me to not make their questions public. People create whole new email accounts so they can email me anonymously. People are afraid of getting these conversations wrong, but they are still trying, and I deeply appreciate that.

These conversations will not be easy, but they will get easier over time. We have to commit to the process if we want to address race, racism, and racial oppression in our society. This book may not be easy as well. I am not known for pulling punches, but I've been occasionally thought of as funny. But it has been very hard to be funny in this book. There is real pain in our racially oppressive system, pain that I as a black woman feel. I was unable to set that aside while writing this book. I didn't feel like laughing. This was a grueling, heart-wrenching book to write, and I've tried to lighten a little of that on the page, but I know that for some of you, this book will push and will push hard. For many white people, this book may bring you face-to-face with issues of race and privilege that will make you uncomfortable. For many people of color, this book may bring forward some of the trauma of experiences around race that you've experienced. But a centuries-old system of oppression and brutality is not an easy fix, and maybe we shouldn't be looking for easy reads. I hope that if parts of this book make you uncomfortable, you can sit with that discomfort for a while, to see if it has anything else to offer you.

Most of the topics you'll find in this book address questions I'm asked most often in my day-to-day work. Some of these are topics that I wish I got more questions about. But these are all things that we need to be able to talk about. I hope that the information provided here, while nowhere near exhaustive, can help provide you with a starting point, to move forward in your discussions with less fear.

Yes, racism and racial oppression in America is horrible and terrifying. The feelings it brings up in us are justified. But it is also everywhere, in every corner of our lives. We have to let go of some of that fear. We have to be able to look racism in the eye wherever we encounter it. If we continue to treat racism like it is a giant monster that is chasing us, we will be forever running. But running won't help when it's in our workplace, our government, our homes, and ourselves.

I am so glad you are here. I am so glad that you are willing to talk about race. I'm honored to be a part of this conversation with you.

one

Is it really about race?

"I MEAN, I JUST FEEL LIKE WE WOULD HAVE GOTTEN further if we'd focused more on class than race."

I'm sitting across from a friend at a coffee shop near my house. He's a good friend—a smart, thoughtful, and well-meaning person. I always enjoy his company and a chance to talk with someone who is also interested in world events. But I'm tired. I'm tired because this is the conversation I've been having since the 2016 election ended and liberals and progressives have been scrambling to figure out what went wrong. What was missing from the left's message that left so many people unenthusiastic about supporting a Democatic candidate, especially against Donald Trump? So far, a large group of people (mostly white men paid to pontificate on politics and current events) seem to have landed on this: we, the broad and varied group of Democrats, Socialists, and Independents known as "the left," focused on "identity politics" too much. We focused on the needs of black people, trans people, women, Latinx people. All this specialized focus divided people and left out working-class white men. That is the argument, anyways.

It's what I and many others have heard throughout the very long presidential campaign; it's what I heard last campaign and the one before that. It's what every other white dude in my political science classes in college had to say.

And although I'm tired, because I have just had this conversation with multiple people for multiple hours the evening before, here I am having it again, hearing what I've always heard: the problem in American society is not race, it's class.

"Surely, if you improve things for the lower classes, you improve things for minorities," he adds, seeing the disappointment and weariness on my face. But I'm going to go ahead and engage in this conversation, because if I can just make some progress with one well-meaning white dude about why class will never be interchangeable with race, I'll feel a little better about our social justice movements.

"If you could do that—if you could improve things for the lower classes—it would," I say, "But how?"

When he then recites the standard recommendations of strengthening unions and raising minimum wages I decide to jump to the point: "Why do you think black people are poor? Do you think it's for the same reasons that white people are?"

This is where the conversation pauses. This is where I see my friend first look at me puzzled and then try to come up with ways to push back. I continue on, since I've already gone this far.

"I live in a world where if I have a 'black sounding' name, I'm less likely to even be called for a job interview. Will I equally benefit from raising minimum wages when I can't even get a job?"

My friend recalls that study, acknowledging that the discrimination I'm referencing is indeed a real thing that happens.

"If I do get a good job and do what society says I should do and save up and buy a house—will I benefit equally when the fact that I live in a 'black neighborhood' means that my house will be worth far less? Will I benefit equally when I'm much more likely to get higher mortgage rates from my bank, or predatory loans that will skyrocket in cost after a few years causing me to foreclose and lose my home and equity and credit, because of the color of my skin?"

I'm on a coffee-and-frustration–fueled roll now.

"If I am able to get what is considered a decent wage for the 'average' American, but my son is locked up in jail like one in three black men are predicted to be, so I'm raising my grandkids on my meager salary, will stronger unions really raise me out of poverty?

"If I'm more likely to be suspended and expelled from school, because even since preschool my teachers are more likely to see my childhood antics as violence and aggression, will a reduction in student loan costs help me when I was pushed out of education before completing high school?"

I'm ranting now, I'm talking fast to get it all out. Not because I'm angry, because I'm not, really. I know it's not my friend's fault that what he's saying is the prevailing narrative, and that it's seen as the compassionate narrative.

But it's a narrative that hurts me, and so many other people of color.

My friend pauses and says, "Well, what are we supposed to do then? Nothing? Can't we focus on this first to get everybody behind it and then address the race stuff?"

To which I sigh and say, "That's the promise that's been made to us for hundreds of years. Those are the words of every labor movement that managed to help white America so much more than everyone else. Those are the words that 'move everybody forward' but in the exact same place, with the exact same hierarchy, and the exact same oppressions. Those words are why the wealth gap between whites and blacks is just as bad as it was when Dr. King was leading marches. We're still waiting. We're still hoping. We're still left behind."

RACE AS WE KNOW IT IN THE US IS CLOSELY INTEGRATED with our economic system. The system of racism functioned primarily as a justification for the barbaric act of chattel slavery and the genocide of Indigenous peoples. You cannot put chains around the necks of other human beings or slaughter them wholesale, while maintaining social rules that prohibit such treatment, without first designating those people as somewhat less than human. And later, the function of racism was somewhat repurposed as a way of dividing lower classes, still with the ultimate goal of the economic and political supremacy of white elites.

Yes, like many say, race is a social construct—it has no bearing in science. Many believe that because race was created by our economic system—because it is a lie told to justify a crime—a unilateral improvement of conditions for lower classes would address the economic and social disparities around race. Money is also a social construct—a series of rules and agreements we all made up while pretending that these pieces of paper are worth our entire lives. But we cannot simply stop thinking of money and it will cease to enthrall us. It has woven its way into every part of our lives. It has shaped our past and our futures. It has become alive.

Race has also become alive. Race was not only created to justify a racially exploitative economic system, it was invented to lock people of color into the bottom of it. Racism in America exists to exclude people of color from opportunity and progress so that there is more profit for others deemed superior. This profit itself is the greater promise for nonracialized people—*you will get more because they exist to get less*. That promise is durable, and unless attacked directly, it will outlive any attempts to address class as a whole.

This promise—*you will get more because they exist to get less*—is woven throughout our entire society. Our politics, our education system, our infrastructure—anywhere there is a finite amount of power, influence, visibility, wealth, or opportunity. Anywhere in which someone might miss out. Anywhere there might not be enough. There the lure of that promise sustains racism.

White Supremacy is this nation's oldest pyramid scheme. Even those who have lost everything to the scheme are still hanging in there, waiting for their turn to cash out.

Even the election of our first black president did not lessen the lure of this promise to draw people to their support of racism. If anything, the election strengthened it. His election was a clear, undeniable sign that some black people could get more, and then what about everyone else's share? Those who had always blatantly or subconsciously depended on that promise, that they would get more because others would get less, were threatened in ways that they could not put words to. But suddenly, this didn't feel like "their country" anymore. Suddenly, they didn't feel like "their needs" were being met.

But aside from that one, mostly symbolic, change of the race of our president, not much else had changed. The promise of racism has still held true: in just about every demographic of socio-political-economic well-being, black and brown people are consistently getting less.

We, people of color, of course are not the only people who have gotten less. Even without the invention of race, class would still exist and does exist even in racially homogenous countries. And our class system is oppressive and violent and harms a lot of people of all races. It should be addressed. It should be torn down. But the same hammer won't tear down all of the walls. What keeps a poor child in Appalachia poor is not what keeps a poor child in Chicago poor—even if from a distance, the outcomes look the same. And what keeps an able-bodied black woman poor is not what keeps a disabled white man poor, even if the outcomes look the same.

Even in our class and labor movements, the promise that you will get more because others exist to get less, calls to people. It tells you to focus on the majority first. It tells you that the grievances of people of color, or disabled people, or transgender people, or women are divisive. The promise that keeps racism alive tells you that you will benefit most and others will eventually benefit . . . a little. It has you believing in trickle-down social justice.

Yes, it is about class—and about gender and sexuality and ability. And it's also, almost always, about race.

Talk about race is inevitable in today's society, but it often doesn't seem to get much farther than an argument about whether or not something is about race. Talk about race can feel like a horribly depressing rendition of "who's on first?" While some argue that these issues of racism must be ad-dressed, others argue that these issues are not race issues, and after much frustration trying to determine whether or not the yet-to-be-had conversation is indeed about race, somebody gives up and walks away, leaving the original issue untouched.

In the day-to-day, determining whether or not an issue is about race can be difficult—not only for white people, but for people of color as well. Rarely is there only one factor or viewpoint in a serious issue. Things are never cut-and-dry. And because we have come up in a society where talking about race is just not something you "do" in polite company, we don't have a lot of practice in putting words to racial issues. But it is difficult, if not impossible, to talk about race when we can't even agree that something is about race. And we have to start somewhere. If you are looking for a simple way to determine if something is about race, here are some basic rules. And when I say basic, I mean basic.

1. It is about race if a person of color thinks it is about race.
2. It is about race if it disproportionately or differently affects people of color.

3. It is about race if it fits into a broader pattern of events that disproportionately or differently affect people of color.

Now, looking at this short list, it's easy to think—hey, that is far too broad, almost *anything* can fall under those categories! And it's true, almost anything can fall under these categories. Why? Because race impacts almost every aspect of our lives. Let's look a little deeper.

It is about race if a person of color thinks it's about race. This may sound at first like I'm asking you to just take every person of color's word for it, as if they are infallible and incapable of lying or misinterpreting a situation. But the truth is, whether or not someone is fallible is beside the point. We are, each and every one of us, a collection of our lived experiences. Our lived experiences shape us, how we interact with the world, and how we live in the world. And our experiences are valid. Because we do not experience the world with only part of ourselves, we cannot leave our racial identity at the door. And so, if a person of color says that something is about race, it is—because regardless of the details, regardless of whether or not you can connect the dots from the outside, their racial identity is a part of them and it is interacting with the situation. Note, if you are a white person in this situation, do not think that just because you may not be aware of your racial identity at the time that you did not bring race to your experience of the situation as well. We are all products of a racialized society, and it affects everything we bring to our interactions.

Something can be about race, and that doesn't mean that it is *only* about race. When I talk about being followed in a store by a white clerk, it is about race, because regardless of the clerk's intention I'm bringing with me my entire history of a black woman who is routinely followed around by staff or security when I shop in stores. This clerk herself may not be thinking of my race at all when she's following me, she may just be an overeager trainee, or maybe she suspects everybody of stealing and follows all customers regardless of race. But she, for her possibly innocent intentions, is also bringing her white identity into the interaction, as someone who is not regularly followed by store personnel and therefore would be unaware of the impact it would have on me to, once again, be followed around a store by a white clerk. She too is making it about race whether she knows it or not. But while this issue is about race and the racial aspects should be addressed, it's also about training—as aggressively following customers of any race is bad business. It can be about all of these things, and it is.

It is about race if it disproportionately or differently affects people of color. Often, when talking about issues of race I will receive messages from white people stating that what I'm talking about is not about race because they, a white person, too suffer from said issue. Poverty cannot be about race if there are poor white people. Incarceration cannot be about race if there are incarcerated white people, and so on. Many white people who themselves often suffer from the same hardships that many people of color suffer from feel erased by discussions of racial oppression.

In contrast, I'll also often hear from white people (often the very same white people) about successful black people that obviously debunk the theory that hardships are race-based. How can poverty be about race if Oprah exists? How can there be lack of representation in the entertainment industry when Beyoncé wins all the awards? Setting aside the fact that the racial exceptionalism of people of color does not detract from, but instead adds to, arguments of racial inequality (because honestly, we don't have to name a few successful white people to argue that they are doing comparatively well in society—there are enough that they don't even stand out), these arguments are a pretty extreme oversimplification of how racial oppression works.

Racial oppression is a broad and cumulative force, it is not a system that puts all its eggs in one basket. And racial oppression will interact with many other privileges and disadvantages to produce a myriad of effects. So yes, you can have a black athlete who won the genetic lottery and combined it with a superhuman amount of dedication and then sprinkle him with a lot of luck and he will turn into a professional superstar earning tens of millions of dollars a year. And yes, you can have a white man born to riches who loses everything he has in the stock market and winds up living in the streets. And you can have a beautiful white woman born with disabilities that set her at a distinct socioeconomic disadvantage, and an able-bodied black woman who was able to claw her way to middle-class comfort, but when it's all tallied up the end result will still show, more often than not, measurably different outcomes for people depending on race. There are very few hardships out there that hit only people of color and not white people, but there are a lot of hardships that hit people of color a lot more than white people.

As I said earlier, just because something is about race, doesn't mean it's only about race. This also means that just because something is about race, doesn't mean that white people can't be similarly impacted by it and it doesn't mean that the experience of white people negatively impacted is invalidated by acknowledging that people of color are disproportionately impacted. Disadvantaged white people are not erased by discussions of disadvantages facing people of color, just as brain cancer is not erased by talking about breast cancer. They are two different issues with two different treatments, and they require two different conversations.

It is about race if it fits into a broader pattern of events that disproportionately or differently affect people of color. When I was in an abusive relationship, it was not just about one incident. It wasn't about the time he called me stupid, or the next time, or the next time. It wasn't about the time he threw our dishes in the trash because he didn't like how I washed them. It wasn't about the time he said he didn't want my friends to come over because he was sure they thought they were better than him. It wasn't about the time that he didn't talk to me for hours because I'd accidentally erased an important message on the answering machine.

Actually, it was about those times, but it wasn't about just one time, it was about all of them. I'd try to talk about it with him, to bring it up. "It's not okay to call me stupid," I'd say. "So I lose my temper once and now I'm abusive?" he'd reply. And before I knew what was happening, I'd be on the defensive, trying to defend my right to a relationship free of abuse. Trying to say that no, calling a person stupid once did not qualify as abuse, but calling a person stupid a few times a week did. To him, it was just an individual incident, and the next abuse was also an individual incident, to be forgotten as quickly as the words left his mouth. To me, it was a daily on-slaught of emotional pain. But whenever I tried to step back and look at the big picture, he'd pull me down to look at a tiny piece: "See this? It's so small. Why would you get upset about this little thing?" I could not address abuse in my rela-tionship because I was too busy defending my right to even call it abuse.

Often, being a person of color in white-dominated society is like being in an abusive relationship with the world. Every day is a new little hurt, a new little dehumanization. We walk around flinching, still in pain from the last hurt and dreading the next. But when we say "this is hurting us," a spotlight is shown on the freshest hurt, the bruise just forming: "Look at how small it is, and I'm sure there is a good reason for it. Why are you making such a big deal about it? Everyone gets hurt from time to time"—while the world ignores that the rest of our bodies are covered in scars. But racial oppression is even harder to see than the abuse of a loved one, because the abuser is not one person, the abuser is the world around you, and the person inflicting pain in an individual instance may themselves have the best of intentions.

Another analogy: imagine if you were walking down the street and every few minutes someone would punch you in the arm. You don't know who will be punching you, and you don't know why. You are hurt and wary and weary. You are trying to protect yourself, but you can't get off this street. Then imagine somebody walks by, maybe gesticulating wildly in interesting conversation, and they punch you in the arm on accident. Now imagine that this is the last straw, that this is where you scream. That person may not have meant to punch you in the arm, but the issue for you is still the fact that people keep punching you in the arm.

Regardless of why that last person punched you, there's a pattern that needs to be addressed, and your sore arm is testimony to that. But what often happens instead is that people demand that you prove that each person who punched you in the arm in the past meant to punch you in the arm before they'll acknowledge that too many people are punching you in the arm. The real tragedy is that you get punched in the arm constantly, not that one or two people who accidentally punched you in the arm might be accused of doing it on purpose. They still contributed to the pain that you have endured—a pain bigger than that one punch—and they are responsible for being a part of that, whether they meant to or not. And if you just punched somebody in the arm that would not be the time to talk about how important it is to protect your right to gesticulate wildly, even if sometimes you accidentally punch people. Once you know that your wild gesticulation is harming people (even if you've been raised to believe that it's your god-given right to gesticulate as wildly as your heart desires without any thought of consequences), you can no longer claim it's an accident when somebody gets hit.

As long as race exists and as long as racial oppression exists, race will touch almost every aspect of our lives. That is not necessarily a bad thing. Race is more than just pain and oppression, it's also culture and history. Personally, my blackness is a history of strength, beauty, and creativity that I draw on every day; it is more that than the history of the horrors that racism has wrought. My blackness has its own language, its own jokes, its own fashion. My blackness is a community and a family and I'm very grateful for it. Humans are resilient and creative beings, and out of a social construct created to brutalize and oppress, we've managed to create a lot of beauty. We can fight racial oppression while still acknowledging and appreciating that.

While just about everything can be about race, almost nothing is completely about race. It is important that we are aware of the different factors in any situation of oppression or conflict (please see the chapter on intersectionality for more very important discussion on this). A lot of people feel like acknowledging race in a problem will make that problem only about race, and that will leave a lot of people out. But race was designed to be interwoven into our social, political, and economic systems. Instead of trying to isolate or ignore race, we need to look at race as a piece of the machine, just as we'd look at class or geography when considering social issues. Race alone is not all you need to focus on, but without it, any solution you come up with just won't work. We live in a complex world, and when looking at socioeconomic problems in our society, we simply cannot come to a viable solution without factoring in race.

We like to filter new information through our own experiences to see if it computes. If it matches up with what we have experienced, it's valid. If it doesn't match up, it's not. But race is not a universal experience. If you are white, there is a good chance you may have been poor at some point in your life, you may have been sick, you may have been discriminated against for being fat or being disabled or being short or being conventionally unattractive, you may have been many things—but you have not been a person of color. So, when a person of color comes to you and says "this is different for me because I'm not white," when you run the situation through your own lived experience, it often won't compute. This is usually where the desire to dismiss claims of racial oppression come from—it just doesn't make sense to you so it cannot be right.

But if you are white, and you are feeling this way, I ask you this: is your lived experience real? Are the situations you've lived through real? Are your interpretations of those situations valid? Chances are, if you are using them to decide whether or not other situations and opinions are valid, you think they are. So if your lived experience and your interpretation of that lived experience are valid, why wouldn't the lived experience of people of color be just as valid? If I don't have the right to deem your life, what you see and hear and feel, a lie, why do you have the right to do it to me? Why do you deserve to be believed and people of color don't?

And if you are a person of color, know this: the world will try to tell you that what you are seeing, hearing, thinking, and feeling is wrong. The world will tell you that you do not know how to interpret what is happening to you and to your community. But you are not wrong, and you have just as much right to be heard and believed as anybody else. If you think it's about race, you are right.

| two |

What is racism?

I T WAS AN ARGUMENT WITH A COWORKER THAT STARTED
where many arguments with coworkers start nowadays,
on the Internet. This coworker had posted a meme about
how poor people should be given drug tests if they want to
get welfare benefits. You know the kind of post I'm talking
about, one that sends a message like "If I need a drug test to
get a hardworking job, you should have one to get the free
stuff my hardworking tax dollars are paying for."

I've seen these memes countless times and they are never
anything less than a gut punch to me. I pointed out that as
someone who had grown up on welfare and was subjected to
this attitude her entire childhood, this sort of stigmatization
really hurts poor people who are just trying to survive. Poor
people shouldn't have to prove how much they deserve to
have a roof over their heads and feed their children.

There are a few ways to react when somebody tells you that your language is unintentionally hurting them. And while I was hoping for a quick apology or maybe just a quick correction, my coworker decided to double down on her claims—and add that she thought that poor people should also be sterilized because "a lot of women take advantage of the system by having more kids to get more money."

Suddenly it was like I was on a TV talk show circa 1984 talking about Welfare Queens. I honestly didn't think that people really believed that myth anymore. A myth that was used to dehumanize a generation of welfare recipients. And, as someone who wouldn't have existed had there been forced sterilization of poor people, I took offense to this comment. In addition, as someone aware of our country's racist history of forced sterilization of women of color, I knew how dangerous statements like these can be.

The discussion became heated quite quickly as my coworker tried to both state that she had not intended to offend me or my brother (who also worked at the same company and was witnessing this argument online), but maybe I needed to be "less angry," because this was why people like me got a bad reputation. Note: "people like you" is a good warning that a conversation is about to head into pretty racist territory. Shit got pretty intense (black-on-black crime was even brought up, I believe), and an entire evening was dedicated to an emotionally draining, and ultimately fruitless, conversation.

The next day, I was talking to a friend about the incident. I was still very upset about what had happened the night before. Believe it or not, I, like most people, really do just want to live in peace and not have four-hour-long arguments about race and poverty on the Internet. And it is always a bit of a gut punch to realize that someone you have been sitting next to for months or even years secretly harbors views that deny your basic humanity as a black woman. No matter how many times it happens, I have yet to get used to it.

"It's really difficult to realize that you've been sitting next to someone capable of racism like that," I explained over coffee.

"Whoa, whoa, whoa, Ijeoma," my friend interrupted, literally putting a hand up to stop me from speaking further, "let's not get ahead of ourselves here."

"Excuse me?" I asked, stunned and confused.

"You can't just go around calling anything racist. Save that word for the big stuff. You know, for Nazis and cross burnings and lynchings. You're just going to turn people off if you use such inflammatory language."

I really *really* wanted this to just be a matter of misunderstanding. I really wanted this to be a case where perhaps he just didn't know how harmful everyday racism is, and once he did, he would change his mind. I tried to explain the real danger of unchecked racism and microaggressions to people of color. But he wasn't going to hear it. There was "real racism" as he defined it, which was a post–reconstruction era horror type of racism, and there was whatever I was talking about (which he wasn't comfortable categorizing but he was pretty sure wasn't that big of a deal)—the day-to-day reminders that I'm less than, that I should just learn to get over or find a more pleasant way to confront. He went on to discuss how his grandma, for example, said some racist things, but she was a kind person and it would be cruel to call a harmless old lady racist and would only make her more racist. It seemed far more important to him that the white people who were spreading and upholding racism be spared the effects of being called racist, than sparing his black friend the effects of that racism.

No matter what I said, no matter how I described the effects that this sort of racism had on me and other people of color, he was not going to accept me using the word "racist" to describe it.

That was when I learned that this was not a friend I could talk to about this really important part of my life. I couldn't be my full self around him, and he would never truly have my back. He was not safe. I wasn't angry, I was heartbroken.

We couldn't talk about the ways in which race and racism impacted my life, because he was unwilling to even acknowledge the racism that was impacting my life and he was unable to prioritize my safety over his comfort—which meant that we couldn't talk about me.

PROBABLY ONE OF THE MOST TELLING SIGNS THAT WE have problems talking about race in America is the fact that we can't even agree on what the definition of racism actually is. Look at almost any discussion of race and racism online, and you'll see an argument pop up over who is racist, who isn't, and who has the right to claim they are suffering from racism. The most common definitions of racism (in my own summation) are as follows: (1) Racism is any prejudice against someone because of their race. Or (2) Racism is any prejudice against someone because of their race, when those views are reinforced by systems of power. While these two definitions

are very close to each other in many ways, the differences between these two definitions of racism drastically change how
you look at and address racism in America.

For the purposes of this book, I'm going to use the second definition of racism: a prejudice against someone based
on race, when those prejudices are reinforced by systems of
power. And this is a definition I recommend you use in your
day-to-day life if your goal is to reduce the systemic harm done
to people of color by racism in America. Let me explain why.

When we use only the first definition of racism, as any prejudice against someone based on race, we inaccurately reduce
issues of race in America to a battle for the hearts and minds
of individual racists—instead of seeing racists, racist behaviors,
and racial oppression as part of a larger system.

There are a lot of individual, unapologetic racists out there.
They're easy to spot—they're the people sharing the Obama =
monkey memes. They are the people sewing swastikas to their
jackets and talking about "White Genocide." This book is not
for them and they are not my primary concern. This book
will not tell you how to get unabashed racists to love people
of color. I'm not a magician. Furthermore, many of those
people have very little real power on their own and tend to
stay on the fringes of society. We, as a society, like our racism
subtler than that. What special power virulent racists do have
can often be thwarted by just staying away from wherever you
see "Obama is a Muslim" signs.

What is important is that the impotent hatred of the virulent racist was built and nurtured by a system that has much
more insidiously woven a quieter, yet no less violent, version
of those same oppressive beliefs into the fabric of our society.

The truth is, you don't even have to "be racist" to be a part of the racist system.

The dude shouting about "black-on-black crime" is reinforced by elected officials coding "problem neighborhoods" and promising to "clean up the streets" that surprisingly always seem to have a lot of brown and black people on them—and end with a lot of black and brown people in handcuffs. Your aunt yelling about "thugs" is echoed in our politicians talking about "super-predators" while building our school-to-prison pipelines that help ensure that the widest path available to black and brown children ends in a jail cell. But a lot of the people voting for stop-and-frisk crime bills or increased security in schools would never dream of blaming racial inequity on "black-on-black crime" or calling a young black man a "thug."

In contrast, a lot of the racists holding "white power" signs aren't even registered to vote. It's the system, and our complacency in that system, that gives racism its power, not individual intent. Without that white supremacist system, we'd just have a bunch of assholes yelling at each other on a pretty even playing field—and may the best yeller win. But there is no even playing field right now. Over four hundred years of systemic oppression have set large groups of racial minorities at a distinct power disadvantage. If I call a white person a cracker, the worst I can do is ruin their day. If a white person thinks I'm a nigger, the worst they can do is get me fired, arrested, or even killed in a system that thinks the same—and has the resources to act on it.

Looking beyond the differences in impact of these two definitions of racism, how we define racism also determines how we battle it. If we have cancer and it makes us vomit, we can commit to battling nausea and say we're fighting for our lives, even though the tumor will likely still kill us. When we look at racism simply as "any racial prejudice," we are entered into a battle to win over the hearts and minds of everyone we encounter—fighting only the symptoms of the cancerous system, not the cancer itself. This is not only an impossible task, it's a pretty useless one.

Getting my neighbor to love people of color might make it easier to hang around him, but it won't do anything to combat police brutality, racial income inequality, food deserts, or the prison industrial complex. THE POLITICAL PROBLEM

Further, this approach puts the onus on me, the person being discriminated against, to prove my humanity and worthiness of equality to those who think I'm less than. But so much of what we think and feel about people of other races is dictated by our system, and not our hearts. Who we see as successful, who has access to that success, who we see as scary, what traits we value in society, who we see as "smart" and "beautiful"—these perceptions are determined by our proximity to the cultural values of the majority in power, the economic system of those in power, the education system of those in power, the media outlets of those in power—I could go on, but at no point will you find me laying blame at the feet of one misguided or even hateful white person, saying, "and this is Steve's fault—core beliefs about black people are all determined by Steve over there who just decided he hates black people all on his own." Steve is interacting with the system in the way in which it's designed, and the end result is racial bigotry that supports the continued oppression of people of color. Systemic racism is a machine that runs whether we pull the levers or not, and by just letting it be, we are responsible for what it produces. We have to actually dismantle the machine if we want to make change.

So a good question to ask yourself right now is: why are you here? Did you pick up this book with the ultimate goal of getting people to be nicer to each other? Did you pick up this book with the goal of making more friends of different races? Or did you pick up this book with the goal of helping fight a system of oppression that is literally killing people of color? Because if you insist on holding to a definition of racism that reduces itself to "any time somebody is mean to somebody of a different race" then this is not the book to accomplish your goals. And those are real and noble goals when we call them what they are—we really should be more kind to each other. But when I look at what is putting me and millions of other people of color at risk, a lack of niceness from white people toward me and people who look like me is very far down the list of priorities.

However, if you came with the second intention—to fight the systemic oppression that is harming the lives of millions of people of color—then you are who I have written this book for. But either way, I encourage you to keep reading, because understanding the truth about racism in America might help you make more friends of different races, too—and they have a better chance of being *real* friends who will feel safe with you.

If you are not yet convinced that the definition of racism as racial prejudice backed by systems of power is the one to go with, I'm fairly confident that the rest of the chapters in this book will do the trick. When reading the subsequent chapters, remember that the concepts and issues discussed in the book were not born from the ether, nor are these racial oppressions the work of a bunch of random white people waking up each morning and saying to themselves, "Today I will do what I can to oppress a person of color" coalescing into the creation of a society with racial disparities of socioeconomic well-being so large and entrenched that they trap multiple generations in the same expectations of success or failure. We live in a society where race is one of the biggest indicators of your success in life. There are sizable racial divides in wealth, health, life expectancy, infant mortality, incarceration rates, and so much more. We cannot look at a society where racial inequity is so universal and longstanding and say, "This is all the doing of a few individuals with hate in their hearts." It just doesn't make sense.

We cannot fix these systemic issues on a purely emotional basis. We must see the whole picture. How do you fix the school-to-prison pipeline on an emotional basis? How do you fix an economic system that values the work done traditionally by white males over that done by women and people of color on an emotional basis? How do you change an education system tailored almost exclusively to the experiences, history, and goals of white families on an emotional basis? How do you address an overwhelmingly white system of government on an emotional basis? We can get every person in America to feel nothing but love for people of color in their hearts, and if our systems aren't acknowledged and changed, it will bring negligible benefit to the lives of people of color.

Furthermore, ignoring the factor of institutional support of racial bias as a component of racism means that we erase the real harm done by that institutional support. When we say, "all racial prejudice is equally harmful," we are denying a large portion of the harm done to people of color and cutting ourselves off from opportunities to repair that harm. But when we acknowledge racism as a part of a system, instead of being limited to our ability to win over racists, we can instead focus on how our actions interact with systemic racism. No, the problem isn't just that a white person may think black people are lazy and that hurts people's feelings, it's that the belief that black people are lazy reinforces and is reinforced by a general dialogue that believes the same, and uses that belief to justify not hiring black people for jobs, denying black people housing, and discriminating against black people in schools.

We have to remember that racism was designed to support an economic and social system for those at the very top. This was never motivated by hatred of people of color, and the goal was never in and of itself simply the subjugation of people of color. The ultimate goal of racism was the profit and comfort of the white race, specifically, of rich white men. The oppression of people of color was an easy way to get this wealth and power, and racism was a good way to justify it. This is not about sentiment beyond the ways in which our sentiment is manipulated to maintain an unjust system of power.

And our emotions, ignorance, fear and hate have been easily manipulated to feed the system of White Supremacy. And we have to address all of this, our emotions, our ignorance, our fear, and our hate—but we cannot ignore the system that takes all of that, magnifies it, and uses it to crush the lives and liberty of people of color to enrich the most privileged of white society.

WHILE ALL OF THE ABOVE MAY MAKE SENSE AS YOU ARE reading it now, I understand that it does little to help in conversations where people are entrenched in their definition of racism that does not consider systems of power. So how do you move forward in discussion of race when accusations of "reverse racism" and "racism against whites" start flying?

First off, understand that this is almost always a defensive reaction to feelings of fear, guilt, or confusion. This is an attempt either to move conversation to a place where the person you are talking to is more comfortable, or to end the conversation completely. ANGER RESSENTMENT ?

Consider restating your intention in engaging in this conversation and ask the person you are talking to to confirm what they are talking about: "I am talking about issues of systemic racism, which is measurably impacting the health, wealth, and safety of millions of people of color. What are you talking about right now?"

Often, if somebody is just trying to use "reverse racism" arguments to shut you down, this is where they will just repeat themselves or claim that you are a hypocrite if you will not shift the conversation instead to the grievances against them that they just decided to bring up. If this happens, it is pretty obvious that you aren't actually having a conversation and it is probably best to walk away and maybe try again later if productive conversation is actually your goal.

But if somebody does want a productive conversation and genuinely believes that being called "cracker" is the same as being called "nigger" and feels angry and invalidated by the insistence that both do not meet your definition of racism, they will say so. This is an educational opportunity. This is a great way to let that person know that you do hear them, and that your experiences do not erase theirs because even though their experience is valid, it is a different experience.

A response I've used is, "What was said to you wasn't okay, and should be addressed. But we are talking about two different things. Being called "cracker" hurts, may even be humiliating. But after those feelings fade, what measurable impact will it have on your life? On your ability to walk the streets safely? On your ability to get a job? How often has the word "cracker" been used to deny you services? What measurable impact has this word had on the lives of white Americans in general?"

In all honesty, from my personal experience, you are still not likely to get very far in that conversation, not right away. But it gives people something to think about. These conversations, even if they seem fruitless at first, can plant a seed to greater understanding.

If you want to further understanding of systemic racism even more among the people you interact with, you can try to link to the systemic effects of racism whenever you talk about racism. Instead of posting on Facebook: "This teacher shouted a racial slur at a Hispanic kid and should be fired!" you can say all that, and then add, "This behavior is linked to the increased suspension, expulsion, and detention of Hispanic youth in our schools and sets an example of behavior for the children witnessing this teacher's racism that will influence the way these children are treated by their peers, and how they are treated as adults." I do this often when I'm talking about racism, and pretty regularly somebody will comment with something like, "That's an aspect of this situation I hadn't considered, thank you."

If you hear someone at the water cooler say, "black people are always late," you can definitely say, "Hey, that's racist" but you can also add, "and it contributes to false beliefs about black workers that keeps them from even being interviewed for jobs, while white workers can be late or on time, but will always be judged individually with no risk of damaging job prospects for other white people seeking employment." That also makes it less likely that someone will brush you off saying "Hey, it's not that big of a deal, don't be so sensitive." PERHAPS

Tying racism to its systemic causes and effects will help others see the important difference between systemic racism, and anti-white bigotry. In addition, the more practice you have at tying individual racism to the system that gives it power, the more you will be able to see all the ways in which you can make a difference. Yes, you can demand that the teacher shouting racial slurs at Hispanic kids should be fired, but you can also ask what that school's suspension rate for Hispanic kids is, ask how many teachers of color they have on staff, and ask that their policies be reviewed and reformed. Yes, you can definitely report your racist coworker to HR, but you can also ask your company management what processes they have in place to minimize racial bias in their hiring process, you can ask for more diversity in management and cultural sensitivity training for staff, and you can ask what procedures they have in place to handle allegations of racial discrimination.

When we look at racism as a system, it becomes much larger and more complicated than it seemed before—but there is also more opportunity to address the various parts of it. And that is what the rest of this book attempts to at least begin to do, chapter by chapter. So now that we know what racism is, let's get to work.

three

What if I talk about race wrong?

WHEN MY WHITE MOTHER GAVE BIRTH TO ME, AND later my brother, in Denton, Texas, she became the subject of a lot of racial commentary in her conservative southern community. But surprisingly, my mother and I had our first really substantive conversation about race late in my life, when I was thirty-four years old. I was well into my career in writing about culture and social justice and my opinions and identity around race were pretty well documented by then. But the truth is, like many families, our conversations growing up mostly revolved around homework, TV shows, and chores.

While I was growing up, my mother had given the obligatory speeches that all parents of black children must give: don't challenge cops, don't be surprised if you are followed at stores, some people will be mean to you because of your beautiful brown skin, no you can't have the same hairstyle as your friends because your hair doesn't do that. But those conversations were one-offs that ceased to be necessary once we were old enough to see the reality of race for ourselves.

Having a white mother, my siblings and I likely had even fewer conversations about race than black children raised by black parents, because there was a lot about our lives that our mother's whiteness made it hard for her to see. My mother loved our blackness as much as was possible for any nonblack person to do, she loved our brown skin, our kinky hair, our full lips, our culture, and our history. She thought we were beauty incarnate.

Our mom never thought that our blackness would hold us back in life—she thought we could rule the world. But that optimism and starry-eyed love was, in fact, born from her whiteness. It was almost impossible for her to see all of the everyday hurdles we had to jump, the tiny cuts of racism that we endured throughout our lives. For our mom, we were black and beautiful and smart and talented and kind—and that's all that mattered. And in the confines of our home, it *was* all that mattered. But as we left home, and our mom began to see us interact as adults with the real world, she began to suspect that there was more to being black in this world than she had previously thought. I could tell that this made my mom uncomfortable, to know that the babies that she had birthed from her own body had entire universes she couldn't see, so the more that my world and my career became focused on race, the less my mom acknowledged it. She just really didn't know what to say.

It was in this context that I received a voicemail from her one evening in 2015. It had the same unnecessary enthusiasm that all my mom's voicemails seem to have, but the topic was definitely new.

"Ijeoma, call me. I've had an epiphany. About race. It's important."

I talk about race for a living, which means I have had a *lot* of uncomfortable conversations on the topic. Quite often, well-meaning white people will attempt to show me how much they "get it" by launching into racial dialogues filled with assumptions, stereotypes, and microaggressions that they are completely unaware of. I have cringed my way through so many of these discussions that you'd think they would have less effect on me. And while that is in some ways true—these conversations have become a bit easier with time—I was in no way ready to have this conversation with my mom. This is not because my mom means any harm or is in any way a worse offender than those who approach me after speaking engagements or readings (she's not), it's just—she's my *mom* and nobody likes to discuss race with their mom.

Here's the thing about my mom, my mom is the kindest, most generous person I've ever known. And she is a wonderful mother and grandmother, beloved by just about all who meet her. But she's also exhausting. My mother does not think before she speaks, nor does she at least take the time to collate her subjects before shouting ten different conversations at you (she refused to get hearing aids for a very long time, so when I say "shouting" I mean shouting). My mom is at times a nonsensical tornado of emotion, enthusiasm, and whimsy. A conversation with her about grocery shopping (which will inevitably wander to a conversation on organic gardening, which will remind her of a joke about potatoes she heard but cannot remember the punchline for) can utilize all of my patience and conversational skills. I love my mom dearly, but I have been rolling my eyes at her for thirty-six years—I am forever a bratty teenager in her presence.

I was trying to think of anything I'd like to do less than call my white mother to hear her epiphany about race, when she did what all mothers do—she immediately called back, and kept calling, until I picked up the phone.

"Did you get my message?" she asked.

"Yes," I sighed, "You had an epiphany?"

"OK," she dove in before I could run away, "So I was telling a joke at work, and it had a black punchline—not like, a punchline *about* black people, but a punchline *for* black people . . . "

This is the part of the conversation where I start cringing. I need you to hear my mom's chipper Kansas accent as she says this.

"*. . . and this coworker of mine, he's black, says, 'What do you know about being black?'*"

This is the part of the conversation where I'm inhaling sharply. I really don't want to know what happens next because I cannot imagine any way that it is good.

"*Like, he was challenging me, you know? Probably thinking, 'this white bitch.'*"

At this point I'm regretting the invention of the telephone.

"*And I was so mad, I was like, this man doesn't know me. He doesn't know what I went through, he doesn't know that I have three black kids.*"

I'm at this point holding the phone a good six inches away from my ear in the hopes that it will make this conversation less painful. Please tell me she didn't actually say these things to this man.

"But then I realized . . . "

Oh no.

" . . . that he's probably gone through so much racism in his life, he doesn't know who the good white people are."

What is she saying? WHAT IS SHE SAYING? HAS SHE NOT READ ANY OF MY WORK? Please let the earth open up and swallow me so I can get out of this conversation.

"And if I were black, I'd probably be really angry all the time, too."

Aaannnd we've now officially entered the worst conversation in the world. I'm talking with my white mom about race. Why can't we be talking about, I don't know—her sex life, or *my* sex life, or my period, or why I'm an atheist—*anything* but this.

"So now I'm not angry at him anymore. I'm just going to go to him tomorrow and explain that I have three black kids and I understand where he's coming from."

And here is where I shouted "NOOOOOOO!" like in those movie scenes where your buddy is about to open a car door that will so obviously set off a bomb that will kill him.

As uncomfortable as this conversation was, it needed to happen. The initial discussion led to a very long talk about race and identity and the differences between being a white mother who has loved and lived with black people, and *being* an actual black person who experiences the full force of a white supremacist society firsthand. She asked if she at least got black credit for doing my hair for all of those years. I said no. She asked why I didn't identify as "part white" when my mother, her, was white. I explained that while I had definitely inherited light-skin privilege due to my mixed heritage I did not feel that whiteness was something that any person with brown skin and kinky hair could inherit, because race doesn't care what your parents look like—just look at all the light-skinned slaves sold away from their black mothers by their white fathers. We talked about how to discuss race without placing undue burden on people of color to educate you. We talked about when to not discuss race (say, in the middle of the workday when your black coworker is just trying to get through a day surrounded by white people). We ended the conversation exhausted and emotional, but with a greater understanding of each other.

After this conversation, the way in which my mom interacted with me changed in ways that I was not expecting. She still calls me to talk about work drama, but also this funny movie she saw, and also perhaps her dream of us all building a cabin in the woods together one day. I still roll my eyes like the thirty-something teenager that I am throughout most of our conversations. But my mom has become more fearless in her support of my work, now that she better understands the role she can play. My blackness is no longer a barrier between us, a symbol of my world that she does not have access to and therefore must avoid fully acknowledging. My mom has shifted her focus on race from proving to black people that she is "down" to pressuring fellow white people to do better.

My mom is now an outspoken advocate for racial equality in her union. And now that the awkwardness has passed, and now that my mom and I have a better understanding of each other, I can talk with her more freely about my life and my work. And while one conversation did not do all of that on its own, it opened up a new way of seeing each other and how we can truly come together as a black daughter and her white mother. So for all its awkwardness, the outcome of that conversation makes me so glad we talked. I'm also glad we talked because I'm pretty sure our conversation stopped my mom from leaving her next conversation with her coworker in tears or being dragged into HR.

NOT ALL OF US ARE LUCKY ENOUGH TO HAVE CONVERSA-tions on race with white people willing to take the emotional risk of investigating the role they play in upholding racism. Not all of us are lucky enough to leave an office discussion on race with no worse than a snide comment and a slightly bruised ego. These conversations, when done wrong, can do real damage. Friendships can be lost, holidays ruined, jobs placed in jeopardy. For this reason, many people avoid the topic of race altogether and recoil when it's brought into conversation.

But you are reading this book because you realize that we *have* to talk about race. Race is everywhere and racial tension and animosity and pain is in almost everything we see and touch. Ignoring it does not make it go away. There is no shoving the four hundred years' racial oppression and violence toothpaste back in the toothpaste tube.

In fact, it's our desire to ignore race that increases the necessity of its discussion. Because our desire to not talk about race also causes us to ignore race in areas where lack of racial consideration can have real detrimental effects on the lives of others—say, in school boards, community programs, and local government. And while it may seem that people of color always need to "put race in everything," it's the neglect of the specific needs of people of color, which exist whether you acknowledge them or not, that necessitate it in the first place.

As a black woman, I'd love to not have to talk about race ever again. I do not enjoy it. It is not fun. I dream of writing mystery novels one day. But I have to talk about race, because it is made an issue in the ways in which race is addressed or, more accurately, not addressed. When my employer enforces hairstyles in their dress code that ignore the very specific hair-style needs of black women (see military restrictions against small braids, for example), then my employer is making race an issue in their attempts to ignore it. When my son's school only has parent-teacher conferences during school hours, they are making race an issue by ignoring the fact that black and Latinx parents are more likely to work the type of hourly jobs that would cause them to lose much-needed pay, or even risk losing their employment altogether, in order to stay involved in their child's education. When I take my kids to movies and none of the characters they see look like them, it's the studio that is making it about race when they decide to make up entire universes in which no brown or black people exist. I just want to go to work, educate my kids, and enjoy a movie.

The truth is, we live in a society where the color of your skin still says a lot about your prognosis for success in life. This is the reality right now, and ignoring race will not change that. We have a real problem of racial inequity and injustice in our society, and we cannot wish it away. We have to tackle this problem with real action, and we will not know what needs to be done if we are not willing to talk about it.

So let's all get a little uncomfortable. If my mom and I can do it, so can you.

YOU'RE GOING TO SCREW THIS UP.

You're going to screw this up royally. More than once.

I'm sorry, I wish I could say that reading this book would guarantee that you'd never leave a conversation about race feeling like you've gotten it all wrong and made everything worse. But I can't. It's going to happen.

It's going to happen, and you should have these conversations anyway.

So now that I've thoroughly bummed you out, let's work on what we can do to lessen the number of times you screw this conversation up, minimize the amount of damage you do, and maximize the benefit to all involved. Here are some basic tips that will increase your chance of conversation success, or at least decrease your chance of conversation disaster:

1) **State your intentions.** Do you know why you are having this particular conversation? Do you know why this matters to you? Is there something in particular you are trying to communicate or understand? Figure it out before moving forward and then state what your intentions are, so that the people you are talking with can determine whether this is a conversation they are willing to join. Very often, these

attempts at conversation fail because two people are entering with two very incompatible agendas and proceed to have two very different conversations, and that doesn't become clear until it blows up in anger and frustration.

2) **Remember what your top priority in the conversation is, and don't let your emotions override that.** If your top priority is understanding racism better, or addressing an incident involving race, or righting a wrong caused by racism, don't let the top priority suddenly become avenging your wounded pride if the conversation has you feeling defensive.

3) **Do your research.** If you are going to be talking about an issue you are not familiar with, a quick Google search will save everyone involved a lot of time and frustration. If terms or subjects come up that you are not familiar with, you can ask for some clarification if you are in person, but know that if you are a white person talking to a person of color—it is never their job to become your personal Google. If you are online and these topics or terms come up, you can Google faster than it takes to hold up the entire conversation begging people to explain things to you. Even if you are a person of color, making sure you understand more about the topic you are trying to address, beyond your immediate experience with it, will give you more confidence in your conversation and will help you get your point across.

4) **Don't make your anti-racism argument oppressive against other groups.** When stressed, when angry,

when tired, or when threatened, our worst selves can come out. It is fine to be angry, there is a lot about racism to be angry about. And it is fine to express that anger. But it is never okay to battle racism with sexism, transphobia, ableism, or other oppressive language and actions. Don't stoop to that level, and don't allow others to. We must be willing to fight oppression in all of its forms.

5) **When you start to feel defensive, stop and ask yourself why.** If you are talking about race and you suddenly feel the need to defend yourself vigorously, stop and ask yourself, "What is being threatened here? What am I thinking that this conversation says about me?" and "Has my top priority shifted to preserving my ego?" If you are too heated to ask yourself these questions, at least try to take a few minutes away to catch your breath and lower your heart rate so that you can. This is something that happens to people of all races, and not only can it stop us from hearing things that need to be said, it can stop us from saying what we really mean to say.

6) **Do not tone police.** Do not require that people make their discussions on the racial oppression they face comfortable for you. See chapter 15 for more details.

7) **If you are white, watch how many times you say "I" and "me."** Remember, systemic racism is about more than individuals, and it is not about your personal feelings. If you find yourself frequently referring to your feelings and your viewpoint, chances are, you are making this all about you.

8) **Ask yourself: Am I trying to be right, or am I trying to do better?** Conversations on racism should never be about winning. This battle is too important to be so simplified. You are in this to share, and to learn. You are in this to do better and be better. You are not trying to score points, and victory will rarely look like your opponent conceding defeat and vowing to never argue with you again. Because your opponent isn't a person, it's the system of racism that often shows up in the words and actions of other people.

9) **Do not force people of color into discussions of race.** People of color live with racism each and every day with no say over when and how it impacts their lives. It is painful and exhausting. When people of color have the rare luxury to choose to not engage in additional dialogue about race, do not deny them that. Even if this discussion is really important to you, you never have a right to demand it. There will be other opportunities.

These tips should help you have more healthy and productive conversations on race and racism. Look through the list and try to recognize where you have had trouble in the past and make a concerted effort to practice the tips that may address where things have gone wrong.

But even with all of your practice, and with the best of your intentions, there will be times where this all goes to shit. There will be times where you truly lose the plot and you aren't sure what has happened, but you do know that you have really messed it up.

It is important to learn how to fail, to learn how to be wrong in a way that minimizes pain to you and others and maximizes what you can learn from the experience. Here are some tips for when your conversation on race has gone very wrong:

1) **Stop trying to jump back in when a conversation is beyond saving**. When things have gone really wrong and everyone is upset, and every additional word feels like a knife in the chest, stop trying to force a resolution. I know that it is very hard to leave an emotional conversation unfinished. It is hard to leave feeling unheard or misunderstood. A resolution can still happen, provided you haven't already burned all the conversational bridges around you, but not right now. It's obvious, by how things have been going, that you are not in a state to find a whole new, productive path for this conversation. Step away, and take some time to calm down. Then think about where things went wrong, and what, if anything, can be done to revisit that conversation later in a productive and healthy way.

2) **Apologize.** If you can see where you screwed up, where you made assumptions, where you got overly defensive, where you hurt someone—own up and say sorry. And mean it.

3) **Don't write your synopsis of this conversation as "the time you got yelled at."** Remember why you had been in this conversation. Remember what the core issue was. Do not revise it in your mind so that

instead of "an important conversation on race that didn't go well," it becomes "that tragic time you got yelled at for trying and felt bad."

4) **Don't insist that people give you credit for your intentions.** If you screwed up and you hurt people, your good intentions won't lessen that hurt. Don't insist that people act less hurt or offended or angry because your intentions were good.

5) **Don't beat yourself up.** Yes, you should feel bad when you say or do something that hurts someone else. And it's natural to feel frustrated when you aren't communicating as effectively as you need to. But you also need to keep in mind that this happens, a lot. If this was something that we were good at talking about, well, I certainly wouldn't have felt the need to write this book. You shouldn't expect those hurt by your actions to just brush what happened aside, but that doesn't mean that you should consider yourself a monster. Instead of drowning in guilt, or ignoring your wrongdoing in order to escape guilt altogether, take some time to really think about what was said and what you could have done better. There is a good chance that the person you were talking to was trying very hard to let you know where you were going wrong. Even if you don't get the chance to make things right with the person you were talking to, you can use what you have learned to make sure you don't screw up in that same way again with other people. You can and will do better if you learn from this experience.

6) **Remember that it is worth the risk and commit to
trying again.** Okay, this conversation didn't go well.
In fact, it went horribly. And now you know that you
have more to learn and more you have to do to get
better at this. But you have to just keep trying, because the alternative is your complacency in the continued oppression of people of color.

No matter what, when you are having a conversation about
racial oppression, you will not be the only one who is nervous and you will not be the only one taking a risk. These
conversations will always be hard, because they will always be
about the hurt and pain of real people. We are talking about
our identities and our histories and the ways in which these
are used and exploited to elevate and oppress. These conversations will always be emotional and loaded to various degrees—and if they are not, then you are likely not having the
right conversation.

Racial oppression should always be an emotional topic to
discuss. It should always be anger-inducing. As long as racism
exists to ruin the lives of countless people of color, it should
be something that upsets us. But it upsets us because it exists,
not because we talk about it. And if you are white, and you
don't want to feel any of that pain by having these conversations, then you are asking people of color to continue to bear
the entire burden of racism alone.

Have these conversations, not just with people of other
races—and I know that's why the majority of you are reading this book. You should be having these conversations with
people of your own race as well. White people—talk about

race with other white people. Stop pretending that you are exempt from the day-to-day realities of race. Take some of the burden of racism off of people of color. Bring it into your life so that you can dismantle racism in the white spaces of your life that people of color can't even reach. People of color, talk to your people about race. Feel the therapeutic effects of honest and safe conversation about race. Examine and confront your internalized racism. Make space to heal and rejuvenate.

Take care in your conversations, remember that you are dealing with the real hurt of human beings. But be brave in that care, be honest in that care. These conversations will never become easy, but they will become easier. They will never be painless, but they can lessen future pain. They will never be risk-free, but they will always be worth it.

four

Why am I always being told to "check my privilege"?

FOR A VERY LONG TIME, SEATTLE WAS A VERY LONELY place for me. I'd spent my entire life here, but it wasn't until my early thirties that I had really found a community.

My entire childhood spent in the working-class suburbs of Seattle had been very isolating. Until high school, my brother and I were almost always the only black kids in class. We had both found small groups of kids who would allow us to hang out in the periphery, but we never really belonged. As we became adults and race shaped more and more of our daily lives and the lives of the white people around us, our racial identity took on "real world" meaning, and isolated us from many of the few friends we'd managed to obtain over the years.

That all changed for me when I was invited to join a Facebook community of people of color in the greater Seattle area.

I was suddenly immersed into a world of black and brown artists, professors, musicians, and tech leaders. We would have hangouts where we'd eat vegan soup and sip fancy cocktails and talk about bold art and systemic oppression and political theory. We put together art showings and community conversations. We had amazing New Year's Eve parties where hundreds of elaborately dressed people of color danced the night away, afros and locs swaying to the beat. It was a dream come true. Suddenly, Seattle didn't seem like the gray city of repressed white comfort that it had previously been. I had found another Seattle—hip, smart, diverse Seattle.

I'd found a home.

We gathered one sunny afternoon for a picnic in the park. Sunny days in Seattle are almost as rare and unpredictable as outsiders think, but somehow, we'd managed to plan this afternoon and carry it off without a raindrop in sight. We met in Capitol Hill, a neighborhood I usually work very hard to avoid—as the overwhelmingly hip white pretentious vibe aggravates my anxiety. This is one of those neighborhoods where upper-middle-class white kids dress up in the same thrifted clothes that branded me a poverty-stricken outcast in school, but become cool when you are thin, white, and financially comfortable. But here we were, more people of color in one tiny park than the entire neighborhood had probably seen in the decades since people of color had been priced out of the neighborhood.

My younger son played with a little girl his age who had bouncy brown curls and a vocabulary far exceeding her six years while I talked with her father, a photographer, about his work. I talked with people on various arts commissions about what shows they were looking forward to seeing this year and the funding they were hoping to provide to community projects. I talked with tech workers about what they were doing to diversify both their staff and the reach of their products. And we chatted about our children, our neighborhoods, our homes. We ate a variety of fancy hummus and salad and drank a fair amount of wine. It was, by any measure, turning into a lovely afternoon.

A few hours into the shindig, a group of black men walked over hesitantly from the basketball courts. They had a look of curiosity on their faces—likely wondering by what magic this large island of picnicking black people had suddenly appeared in the middle of this ocean of whiteness.

"Hey, what are y'all—some kind of group? What are you doing out here?" one of the men asked.

"We're a community of people of color in Seattle and we're having a picnic."

The man scanned the spread of people, appetizers, and wine and nodded, "Can we join you?"

Almost all conversation in the group came to a stop and an uncomfortable silence took its place.

At first I didn't know why. But then I knew. These were black people, but they were definitely not *with us.* They had a different style, a different swagger than ours. They were close-cropped fades and basketball shorts, we were long locs and hipster jeans. These were people who came to this white-dominated part of town simply for the well-maintained basketball court. We came for the gastro-pubs and art walks and a lot of us lived here. These were people that would have been called "real black" by people I grew up with who often used such terms to point out how "not black" my education, speech, and fashion sense obviously made me.

"Sure," the organizer said, and handed up a bottle of wine. The awkwardness was eased and the men sat down and joined us. Conversation resumed as it had before, and after an hour or so, I gathered my kid and my picnic blanket and went home.

In the following days I couldn't stop thinking about those men who had approached us at the picnic. I couldn't stop thinking about the silence of our group as they walked up. Why had it been so awkward? Why would our own people, fellow people of color, make us so uncomfortable?

And then I realized why with a sinking feeling to my stomach. When we were building our community, those men weren't who we had in mind as members. When we talked about expanding art opportunities for people of color in Seattle, they weren't who we had in mind. When we talked about diversity in tech, they weren't who we had in mind. When we talked about getting a hip group of black and brown people together for a picnic on a sunny day, they weren't who we had in mind. When we talked about community, they weren't who we had in mind.

And this wasn't because we felt any animosity towards these men, it was because when we talked about people of color, we talked about *people like us*. We were talking about people of color with college degrees, and "high-fashion" clothes and eclectic tastes in music. We talked about people in our social groups with our interests and our opportunities and struggles. We talked about yes, people of color all facing oppression due to the color of our skin, and many due to our genders and sexuality—but we were also talking about people with our specific sets of privilege.

And we hadn't examined that.

And it smacked us right in the face when a group of fellow people of color walked up to us and we immediately knew that they weren't invited. And what sucks is that they could have been all of these things—they could have been tech engineers or artists or lovers of eclectic music and this entire awkwardness could have been built off of nothing more than assumption and stereotype, or they could have had completely opposite interests and circumstances, but no matter what, they still would have been our people. But we didn't see them, because they simply hadn't occurred to *us*.

I then realized that there was a distinct set of my black friends who I had never seen at any of this group's events, even though just about every person of color in town was aware that the group existed. I began to ask some of them why they hadn't been around.

"Too pretentious," some said.

"I just don't really feel like I belong," said others.

"Nah, those are some bougie black folk," said a black woman I had dated.

I began to see how unaware of our privilege our group had been. We had been patting ourselves on the back for creating this great community, for creating a home for people of color in a hostile city—and our unexamined privilege had kept out those most negatively impacted by overwhelmingly white, wealthy Seattle—those who, unlike us, could not cushion some of the blows of racism with at least some of the indicators of success that white Seattle valued. Yes, we had worked very hard for what we had been able to accomplish, but we'd also been very lucky. But we forgot the luck and wore our status as a symbol of pride—creating a hierarchy in a group in desperate need of solidarity. And no, I'm not saying that those men who approached us at the park needed us to save them or embrace them, but if we weren't going to be there for and with *all* people of color, we should probably at least stop pretending to be creating a radical space of acceptance and just admit that we were simply a social club for comfortable people of color.

That group has grown and changed over the years, and I don't really know if it's still as privileged or ignorant of its privilege as it once was. I'm not nearly as involved with it as I used to be. It is not what I'm seeking anymore. I wouldn't call it disillusionment—at least not with the group. It's an amazing and much-needed space for many who are often made to feel alone. But that one afternoon in the sun definitely brought about a disillusionment with myself and what type of black woman I thought I was, and caused me to question my individual work and change my focus to ensure that when I talk about black people, I'm talking, as best as I can while acknowledging the limitations of my own life experience, about *all* black people—of all classes, all education levels, all genders, all sexualities, and all abilities. And once I shifted that focus, my community opened up to me in ways that I never thought possible.

I DON'T KNOW IF THERE'S ONE PHRASE MORE MALIGNED in social justice language than "check your privilege." It is a phrase most likely to be met with dismissal and derision. It's a phrase viewed as an ineffective weapon hurled at someone with no other purpose than to win an argument or at least silence opposition. Often people will preempt requests to check said privilege in heated social justice conversations by saying, "I bet this is where you tell me to check my privilege" with the eye-roll–filled sarcasm seeping through. But as disliked as the phrase "check your privilege" is, I've found from my conversations and from witnessing the conversations of others that very few people actually know what privilege is, let alone how they would go about checking it.

It is a shame that so much derision has been heaped upon a concept that so few people understand—especially one as important as privilege. Not only is the concept of privilege integral to our real understanding of issues of race in the West, it is crucial to the success of any efforts towards social justice that we make.

So what is privilege? Is it, as many fear, "good shit you should feel bad about having so that other people can feel better about not having it?" No, it's not. But that isn't to say that understanding privilege won't make you feel bad. It might make you feel very bad, and I'm convinced that is why so many of us are quick to dismiss discussions on privilege before they even get started. We may not fully "get" privilege, but we have a feeling that understanding our privilege will change what we feel about ourselves and our world, and not in a good way.

The definition of privilege is in reality much simpler than a lot of social justice discussions would have you believe. Privilege, in the social justice context, is an advantage or a set of advantages that you have that others do not.

These privileges are not due 100 percent to your efforts (although your hard work may indeed have helped), and the benefits of these privileges are disproportionately large or at least partially undeserved when compared to what the privilege is for. These advantages can often be ascribed to certain social groups: privilege based on race, physical ability, gender, class, etc. But these privileges can also lie in areas that you may have not considered, like sexuality, body type, and neurological differences. It is in these advantages and their coupled disadvantages that the health and well-being of large amounts of people are often determined. If we are truly dedicated to addressing systemic oppression and inequality, we must understand the full impact of these advantages and disadvantages in order to move toward real change in our society and ourselves.

Let's use a bit of my privilege as an example: I have a college degree in political science. I worked very hard for my degree, studying at all hours of the night while also taking care of a small child. I probably worked harder than many of the other students in my class, being the only black female single parent there. I also worked hard to get into college in the first place, maintaining my grades while working every evening to help my single mom make ends meet. I'm proud of my degree and the effort that I put into it. While I do have a right to be proud of my degree, it would be dishonest of me to pretend that this degree is 100 percent owed to my efforts. I was raised by a college-educated mother who taught me that a degree was important. I grew up as a neuro-typical, nondisabled child whom school was designed to serve and for whom teachers were willing and trained to dedicate their time and efforts. My grade school education was free and open to people of all genders and economic classes. I had enough security in my home and nutrition as a child to be able to concentrate on my studies. I live in a country that provides at least some college grants and loans. I grew up in an area that allows and supports the advanced education of women. I did not have to drop out of school to help support my family. I am a documented citizen and therefore eligible for financial aid. These are just some of the many ways in which privilege helped me get my college degree. To look at this list and say, "anybody could do this if they just work hard enough" would be a lie.

Some of the benefits that I've received from my degree are also not what the degree, in itself, has earned. Benefits that should go with my degree are things like being more qualified for a job in politics, government, or social services. Also the ability to yell, "I HAVE A DEGREE IN POLIT-ICAL SCIENCE!" during arguments about politics. I get a well-earned warm feeling when I stare at my diploma. I get to talk about my degree in political science in this book. That's about $30k in benefits, right? Right? If you can think of any more, please email me because it would make me feel a lot better about these student loans I'm still paying. But there are some benefits to my degree that are, well, let's say they're "problematic." Yes, my degree makes me more qual-ified for jobs that utilize my political science knowledge, but that degree—any degree—made me eligible for management positions in the marketing and tech fields I've worked in, while more talented coworkers without a degree were auto-matically disqualified. Yes, I do deserve to feel proud of my degree, but it isn't deserving of the general reputation that

I, as a college graduate, am a smarter, more responsible, and more valuable citizen than those without a degree (especially when you consider all the advantages listed above that helped make my degree accessible to me). My degree has also gotten me higher pay than other people of color that I worked with in just about every job I've held in my adult life, and I've never worked in a field (until perhaps now, as a writer) that has even mildly utilized my political science skills. All of these advantages, for a status that I didn't fully earn, set me higher up in a socioeconomic hierarchy than others, and place other people below.

If I were to go along thinking that my degree was 100 percent due to my efforts and all the benefits that I received were 100 percent deserved, it would then require that I think that those who did not benefit deserved to not benefit—say, an otherwise qualified coworker of mine who was exempt from the promotion I received because he did not have a degree. Because my advantage over that coworker helped me and hurt him, I would have to buy into the entire system in order to believe that it was 100 percent deserved. I would accept my promotion thinking that it was rightfully mine, and then I would promote other people, using their degree as one of the deciding factors, thinking that it rightfully indicated that they deserved the promotion—even if that degree had nothing to do with the position I was hiring for. I would then be perpetuating the same advantages and disadvantages—or system of privilege—on other people. I would be part of the reason why the deck was stacked against those who were unable, for so many reasons, to get a college degree. In a fair competition truly based on skill and experience, I may have still gotten that promotion. I may well have been the most qualified person for the job. But it wasn't a fair competition, and in acting like it was fair, and accepting my prize without question, I helped ensure that it would stay unfair.

This right here, the realization that we may be a part of the reason why the deck is stacked against others, that we may have been contributing to it for years without our knowledge, is why the concept of privilege is so threatening to so many. We don't want to think that we are harming others, we do not want to believe that we do not deserve everything we have, and we do not want to think of ourselves as ignorant of how our world works. The concept of privilege violates everything we've been told about fairness and everything we've been told about the American Dream of hard work paying off and good things happening to good people. We want to know that if we do "a" we can expect "b," and that those who never get "b" have never done "a." The concept of privilege makes the world seem less safe. We want to protect our vision of a world that is fair and kind and predictable. That reaction is natural, but it doesn't make the harmful effects of unexamined privilege less real.

When somebody asks you to "check your privilege" they are asking you to pause and consider how the advantages you've had in life are contributing to your opinions and actions, and how the lack of disadvantages in certain areas is keeping you from fully understanding the struggles others are facing and may in fact be contributing to those struggles. It is a big ask, to check your privilege. It is hard and often painful, but it's not nearly as painful as living with the pain caused by the unexamined privilege of others.

You may right now be saying "but it's not my privilege that is hurting someone, it's their lack of privilege. Don't blame me, blame the people telling them that what they have isn't as good as what I have." And in a way, that is true, but know this, a privilege has to come with somebody else's disadvantage—otherwise, it's not a privilege. As a light-skinned black woman, I'm viewed by many in society as more intelligent and less threatening than darker-skinned black people. This is a privilege, because in order to be viewed as "more intelligent" others have to be viewed as "less intelligent." If black people of all shade ranges were viewed as equally intelligent until proven otherwise by their actions, then that privilege would cease to exist. But when somebody treats me as "more intelligent" and treats a darker-skinned black person as "less intelligent," if I don't challenge that, if I just accept the unearned compliment (and the better grade, the job offer, the access to more financially successful areas of society) with a smile and don't ask why it was given to me or why it's not also given to my darker-skinned counterparts—I'm benefitting from unfair privilege and helping perpetuate it further. The darker-skinned person does not really have much power to challenge that privilege—who would listen to her when they already consider her less intelligent? If I want to live in a world where shadeism (a byproduct of racism creating a hierarchy within minority races based on skin tone) doesn't exist, I have to do my part by confronting it whenever I encounter it—even if it means less benefits for me and some uncomfortable conversations.

When we are willing to check our privilege, we are not only identifying areas where we are perpetuating oppression in order to stop personally perpetuating that oppression, but we are also identifying areas where we have the power and access to change the system as a whole. Where I benefit most from being able-bodied is where I have the most power and access to change a system that disadvantages disabled people. Where I benefit most from being cisgender is where I have the most power and access to change a system that disadvantages transgender people. When we identify where our privilege intersects with somebody else's oppression, we'll find our opportunities to make real change.

So yes, we all need to be checking our privilege. And not just when we are told to in the middle of an argument. I recommend practicing looking for your privilege at first when you are in a neutral situation. Sit down and think about the advantages you've had in life. Have you always had good mental health? Did you grow up middle class? Are you white? Are you male? Are you nondisabled? Are you neuro-typical? Are you a documented citizen of the country you live in? Did you grow up in a stable home environment? Do you have stable housing? Do you have reliable transportation? Are you cisgender? Are you straight? Are you thin, tall, or conventionally attractive? Take some time to really dig deep through all of the advantages that you have that others may not. Write them down.

You may well want to list your disadvantages as well. This is not the time for that, so please resist the urge. It is natural to feel like focusing on your advantages invalidates your disadvantages and your struggles in life, but that is not what will happen. You can be both privileged in some areas of life, and underprivileged in others. Both can be true at once and can impact your life at the same time. This is an exercise you should do even if you feel extremely underprivileged in life. I feel very underprivileged as a black, queer woman, and it would be easy to dismiss calls to check my own privilege under the argument that it's really those with a lot of privilege who should be doing the work and I'm too busy fighting racism and sexism to fight the few advantages I do have. But failing to check my own privilege means that my efforts to fight racism and sexism would leave out many of the women and people of color I claim to be fighting for. I march for black people, but am I marching for black trans women, disabled black people, incarcerated black people as well? The number of people I'd be leaving behind and continuing to oppress by refusing to check my privilege would make my efforts ineffective at best and harmful at worst. If thinking about your privilege without addressing your oppression is hard for you, and you need to write down your lack of privilege later, that is fine. But please, dedicate this time to seeing how you can make your understanding of justice and equality more inclusive.

Once you've written down a nice long list of privilege, start thinking about how this privilege might have influenced not only your status in society, but your experience with and understanding of the world at large. How might your privilege have impacted your ideas on racism, on education, on the environment? Then start seeking out work on these subjects by people who don't have your same privilege, and listen when those people are speaking. Being privileged doesn't mean that you are always wrong and people without privilege are always right—it means that there is a good chance you are missing a few very important pieces of the puzzle.

Practice this often, especially when thinking about social or political issues. After having practiced looking at my privilege more formally, I casually revisit this exercise whenever I'm confronted with a new privilege that I was previously unaware of, and again at the start of every year, as a way to refocus on my social justice goals. Get used to that uncomfortable feeling that arises when you discover that perhaps your privilege is hindering your ability to truly understand or address an issue. Get used to that pang of guilt that comes with realizing yet another area of life where you've benefited at the expense of others. It will not kill you. You can withstand it. You want to be more comfortable with this, so that when you are confronted with your privilege in a stressful situation (like a Facebook argument that suddenly takes a turn for the worse) you will be able to limit your defensiveness enough to listen and learn.

This will also help you better empathize with the feelings of anger, fear, and shame that people feel when confronted with their privilege and may help you approach someone about their privilege with more generosity. It is also easier to explain privilege to someone else, if you should choose to do so, if you are familiar with explaining it to yourself. When you first became aware of an area of your privilege, it did not appear to you as "privilege." You had to be able to see what your advantage was, that others did not have that advantage, and that it was influencing your words and decisions in a way that could be harming others. Remembering this might allow you to put more detail into your entreaties for people to check their privilege and may increase the chances they will actually try. No, you do not owe someone who is oppressing you with their unexamined privilege any particular kindness or education, but know that you have unexamined privilege too, no matter how woke you think you are—and someone will be telling you to check your privilege while you try to battle your own defensiveness as you figure out what the hell they are talking about.

If someone confronts you with your privilege from a place of anger or even hatred, if someone does not want to take the time or does not have the emotional energy to further explain to you where your privilege lies, know that it is still a kindness. Try to remember that the alternative to not being made aware of your privilege (no matter how it may sting) is your continued participation in the oppression of others. Someone is giving you an opportunity to do better, no matter how unpleasant the delivery. Thank them.

Once you are aware of your privilege, you can get to work on dismantling it. This is where checking your privilege really pays off. Here are some examples of where you can find both privilege and opportunities to help create change in your day-to-day life:

- Does your privilege mean that you are more likely to sit in a manager's meeting while others are not? Ask why there are no disabled people in the room.
- Does your privilege mean that politicians are begging for your political support? Ask what they are going to do for people of color next time they knock on your door to hand you a flier.
- Were you able to get a fancy private education as a child? Use your resulting financial security to support levies to improve public schools.

- Don't have to juggle work and children? Use the promotion that added flexibility helped you get to support employer-funded childcare and family leave programs.
- Have the schedule flexibility to attend a PTA meeting? At your next meeting, ask them to move future meeting times to hours that more working parents can attend and give parents other ways to contribute if they can't be there.

The possibilities of where you can leverage your privilege to make real, measurable change toward a better world are endless. Every day you are given opportunities to make the world better, by making yourself a little uncomfortable and asking, "who doesn't have this same freedom or opportunity that I'm enjoying now?" These daily interactions are how systems of oppression are maintained, but with awareness, they can be how we tear those systems down.

So please, check your privilege. Check it often.

five

What is intersectionality and why do I need it?

"I'M SO SORRY," I SAID AS MY PHONE BUZZED AGAIN, "Can you excuse me for a minute? I have this—thing I need to take care of with my kids really quick."

My dinner companion graciously nodded in reply and I rushed upstairs to my hotel room, to my laptop. "Come on . . . come on . . . " I said to myself as I tried to quickly run the online program. I knew that every minute this took made me more and more rude, and more and more a liar. No, there was no issue with my kids, and yes, it's pretty shitty to use them as an excuse (hey, consider it a rare indulgence for single parents). But I was damned if I was going to say, "Sorry, I have to leave our dinner to go run a program to block thousands of Twitter trolls who think I hate black men before this shit goes viral and I can never use Twitter again." There's no rescuing dinner after that.

It had started quietly enough weeks earlier. I had found out that a famous black male musician was coming to town to perform. This musician (who shall remain nameless) was long believed by many, including myself, to be a sexual predator of multiple young black women and teenage girls. How could a man so notorious for suspicion of such heinous offenses sell out an arena in liberal Seattle? How was this man still rich and famous? I tweeted out some of my frustration, expressing the desire that, if he'd never see jail time due to a society that did not value black womanhood, he would at least be forever reminded of his misdeeds in any venture he tried to undertake. Plus a lot of swear words. I was angry. I really care about the plight of black women and girls. The Tweets got some likes and a few retweets, but, as I said, society doesn't really value black womanhood, and the conversation didn't gain much traction.

That is, until, Hotep Twitter got hold of my Tweets. To Hotep Twitter (think black men's rights activists with the added fun of wildly inaccurate Egyptian origin mythology, on Twitter), the fact that I would use so many swear words on a black man accused of assaulting multiple young black women led them to only one conclusion: I hated black men.

Not only did I hate black men, but I was on the side of the lynch mobs, on the side of the school-to-prison pipeline. I was the house Negro, the high-yellow bed wench who'd spread her legs for her white master (for real, these are words that have been sent to me). And before I knew what was happening, I had thousands of angry black men (and some black women) interrupting my dinner with buzzes on my phone notifying me that they were working as hard as possible to drown my Twitter feed in hatred.

To those clamoring to send me hateful messages, I had betrayed black people with my comments against a black musician. I had taken the side of white oppressors by speaking so publicly about a black man's crimes. But this is because their idea of blackness and the oppressions that black people face did not include black women and the specific oppressions we face from being both black *and* women. While they were fighting to defend this black man, they were giving little thought to his black female victims or the other black women who may have been harmed by seeing someone so widely known for harming black women lauded so publicly. This sort of hurtful denial of the various oppressions that I and many others have to navigate is something I'm often forced to confront—in office meetings, in social justice forums, in feminist activist groups, in government and social programs aimed at fighting inequality—and, most often, on the Internet.

I'd seen the consequences of this sort of anger at people who demand that their various identities be taken into account when discussing larger social groups and I'd seen how quickly this anger can turn into a full-scale online mob. I'd seen how these campaigns of harassment can take on a life of their own; lasting weeks, months—even years. I knew that it could lead to doxxing campaigns, where angry Internet vigilantes publish your home address and work info to the masses. I knew that there was a limited amount of time to contain this problem before there would be no saving my online presence and I'd have to leave my Twitter account for dead. Twitter may seem to many like a frivolous thing to be in a panic over, but it is not just a fun online community for me. Twitter is a huge part of my job. As a black woman, it is very hard to build a platform for your writing in a white male–dominated industry that shows little interest in giving black women regular columns or placing them behind a news anchor's desk. Twitter is a huge tool in finding and maintaining my audience, and it is how many editors who want to commission the work of women of color find me. I simply could not afford to be pushed off of that platform. I scrambled to block as many of these attackers as I could in an attempt to stem this assault in as much time as I felt I could be away without worrying my very patient dinner companion too much or making her feel abandoned. Then I closed my laptop, said an atheist prayer for the best, and went back downstairs to apologize and finish dinner.

By the next day, the uproar had mostly died down. I'd been able to cut off access to my account to a large number of Twitter users that online instigators were hoping to send to my page to harass me. When the return on troll investment (the barrage of hate met with my frantic pleas and denials) had proved underwhelming, the bullies had moved on.

I breathed a sigh of relief at the crisis averted. But then I was almost as quickly overcome with sadness. All I had done was express anger at the abuse of black women, all I had done was ask people to care about us as they did about others. All I had done was ask for the fight for black lives to include black women, too, and for that, I had to block tens of thousands of black people—my people—who wanted me to pay for my audacity.

And I, like so many other prominent black women on social media, felt very alone and very abused. Because in our struggle for justice and equality, we are often exploited and discarded. White women will heap praise on my words calling for the destruction of the patriarchy, and then turn around and ask why I have to "be so divisive" or say dismissively that I "sound like Al Sharpton" when I dare bring up race. Black men will follow me by the dozens after each essay I write calling out White Supremacy, but will forget all of that and call me a "feminist tool of slave masters" when I demand that black women be treated with respect and dignity by everyone—even black men. And even though Black Lives Matter was founded by black women, even though black women have been at the heart of every feminist movement in this country's history—nobody marches for us when we are raped, when we are killed, when we are denied work and equal pay. Nobody marches for us.

Intersectionality, the belief that our social justice movements must consider all of the intersections of identity, privilege, and oppression that people face in order to be just and effective, is the number one requirement of all of the work that I do. When I first learned about intersectionality in college, I honestly had no idea what a huge part of my life it would later become. What was at first an interesting if not abstract theory I wrote about for college papers became a matter of my political, social, spiritual, and yes, even physical survival. Because I am not capable of cutting myself to pieces. I'm not capable of cutting away my blackness in order to support feminism that views the needs of women of color as divisive inconveniences. I'm not capable of cutting away womanhood in order to stand by black men who prey on black women. I'm a black woman, each and every minute of every day—and I need you to march for me, too.

WHILE THIS BOOK IS ABOUT RACE, I'M SURE YOU KNOW that we as people are far more than just our race. But even further, our experience of race is shaped by far more than just our skin color and hair texture. And just as racial identity is not the only type of identity in our society, racial oppression is not the only form of oppression in our society. Racial privilege is not the only form of privilege in our society.

Each of us has a myriad of identities—our gender, class, race, sexuality, and so much more—that inform our experiences in life and our interactions with the world. As we saw when we were checking our privilege, the different hierarchies, privileges, and oppressions assigned to these identities affect our lives in many ways. These privileges and oppressions do not exist in a vacuum, however, and can combine with each other, compound each other, mitigate each other, and contradict each other.

We walk through the world with all our identities at once and therefore our day has an endless number of possible combinations of outcomes depending on how individual events and situations we encounter interact with our individual identities.

I'm a black, queer woman. If I'm harassed on the street, I don't know if it is because I'm black, if it's because I'm a woman, or if it's because I'm queer. In fact, it may be all three reasons at once. But many of our social justice movements would fail to consider the ways in which our multiple identities interact, or intersect (for example, when feminist groups are discussing how to fight the street harassment of women).

As a black, queer, middle-class woman, my queer identity may often be overlooked by anti-racist or feminist movements; my female identity may be overlooked by anti-racist or queer movements; my black identity may be overlooked by feminist or queer movements; and my middle-class identity may well cause me to overlook poor people in all movements. And when that happens, none of them can really help me or many others.

This is very often the case in our movements, and our society at large. Feminist movements, for example, often fail to consider the different needs and challenges that many women of color face when they differ from what white women face. I've done a fair amount of work in support of reproductive rights, and I'm still surprised at how often reproductive rights groups claim that they are fighting for reproductive rights for all women, yet consistently ignore the documented racial bias in the medical field that keeps many women of color from accessing reproductive healthcare, regardless of law.

So how does this happen? How do our social justice efforts so often fail to help the most vulnerable in our populations? This is primarily a result of unexamined privilege. Because of how rarely our privilege is examined, even our social justice movements will tend to focus on the most privileged and most well represented people within those groups. Anti-racism groups will often tend to prioritize the needs of straight men of color, feminist groups will tend to prioritize the needs of white women, LGBTQ groups will tend to prioritize the needs of white gay cisgender men, disability rights groups will tend to prioritize the needs of disabled white men. Imagine where this leaves a disabled Latinx trans woman on any group's priority list. Because the needs of the most privileged are usually the ones prioritized, they are often the only ones considered when discussing solutions to oppression and inequality. These solutions, not surprisingly, often leave the underprivileged populations in our movements behind.

The idea of intersectionality provides a more inclusive alternative to the status quo. Coined by the brilliant race theorist and civil rights activist Kimberlé Crenshaw in 1989, the term "intersectionality" was born from Crenshaw's work to shed light on the ways in which experiences in both race and gender intertwine to uniquely impact the lives of black women and women of color. Crenshaw referred to those intersections of race and gender as intersectionality and stressed the need to consider intersectionality in our social justice movements.

Intersectionality as a theory and practice was quickly adopted by prominent black feminists to describe the need they saw for a more holistic view of race and gender. From there intersectionality spread to a large section of feminist scholarship and activism and was expanded to include class, ability, and sexuality as well.

Intersectionality, and the necessity of considering intersectionality, applies to more than just our social justice efforts. Our government, education system, economic system, and social systems all should consider intersectionality if they have any hope of effectively serving the public.

Intersectionality helps ensure that fewer people are left behind and that our efforts to do better for some do not make things far worse for others. Intersectionality helps us stay true to our values of justice and equality by helping to keep our privilege from getting in our way. Intersectionality makes our systems more effective and more fair.

So if intersectionality makes all of our social justice efforts so much better, why isn't it a more prominent part of our social justice movements? I believe there are many reasons that may be why social justice movements have been slow to adopt intersectional practices:

- **Intersectionality slows things down.** The simple truth is, when you are only considering the needs of a select few, it's a lot easier to make what looks like progress than when you have to consider the needs of a diverse group of people. This is where you often hear people say things like, "Well, let's just work on what the majority needs first and we'll get to the rest later."

- **Intersectionality brings people face-to-face with their privilege.** People, in general, do not like to recognize the ways in which they may be unfairly advantaged over other people. To embrace intersectionality is to also embrace the knowledge of those advantages and to acknowledge that your advantages may have kept you from first seeing the disadvantages others face. This becomes even stickier in social justice movements where you are targeting oppression. When you are supposed to be fighting the evils of "the man" you don't want to realize that you've become "the man" within your own movement.

- **Intersectionality decentralizes people who are used to being the primary focus of the movements they**

are a part of. If your needs have always been among the prioritized in your social justice movements, that is going to feel like the natural order of things for you. It may well have not even occurred to you that others within your movement have never felt prioritized. While you may, in theory, want others to have equal priority within your movements, when put into practice, that does mean less time and attention for your specific needs—and that can feel really unfair, even if it isn't.

- **Intersectionality forces people to interact with, listen to, and consider people they don't usually interact with, listen to, or consider.** People like to form groups with people they consider "similar" to themselves. Many of us spend a lot of our days with "people like us"—people with similar backgrounds, goals, identities, and personalities. This is human nature. This also means that our social justice efforts often self-segregate in this way as well. Intersectionality requires that we break free from these divides and reach out to people we have not reached out to in the past. While many people would not consider this unpleasant, it is often uncomfortable—at least at first.

These challenges to intersectionality are not easy to overcome, but it is worth the effort. I strongly believe that the vast majority of people who set out to fight racism, sexism, ableism, and other forms of oppression do so because they really do want to make the world a better place for all people. But if you don't embrace intersectionality, even if you make progress for some, you will look around one day and find that you've become the oppressor of others.

So how do you increase the intersectionality in your discussions of race? Here are some questions to ask yourself:

- **How might race, gender, sexuality, ability, class, or sex impact this subject?** You don't have to have the exact answers to this question, but asking it of yourself will give you ideas of other viewpoints to seek out.
- **Could the identity differences between me and the person I'm talking with about race be contributing to our differences of opinion or perspective?**
- **Are the people in my racial justice conversations and the opinions being considered truly representing the diversity of identities that interact with the subject matter being addressed?**
- **Does my scholarship of racial justice reflect the diversity of identities impacted by racial oppression?** Who writes the books and articles I'm using to help inform my opinions?
- **Am I listening to people whose identities and experiences differ from mine?**
- **Am I looking for what I don't know?** Am I asking people if they notice anything missing from my racial justice efforts?
- **Am I shifting some focus and power away from the most privileged in the conversation?** Am I letting those we don't hear from very often speak first? Am I making conversation accessible to everyone who wants to participate? Am I prioritizing the opinions of those who are often overlooked?

- **Am I providing a safe space for marginalized people to speak out?** If you find yourself saying, "Well, disabled people never talk to me about this" or, "I just never hear from black women," then you need to ask yourself why and what you can do to make people feel safe to speak up around you. Privilege has been used to silence people for so long, that you will need to put out the effort to let people know that you will value and respect their input. Don't expect that trust to form immediately with your intentions.

It's not enough for you to personally believe in intersectionality. We need to start demanding intersectionality of all those who seek to join us in our social justice movements. If you want to call attention to the need for greater focus on intersectionality in your discussions of race and racial justice efforts, here are some things to remember:

- **Most people don't know what intersectionality is, and unknown words can put people on the defensive.** You may need to explain further, with examples of the intersecting identities not being considered, if you don't want people to just pretend like they understand but then never put intersectionality into practice.
- **It's often best to start first with real-life examples of how this conversation or project could be more intersectional.**
- **The concept of intersectionality is more easily understood when viewed as an opportunity to do better**

and do more, instead of just an examination of the ways in which these efforts are failing.

- **Intersectionality is absolutely always important to all discussions of race and social justice; do not let other people bully you out of prioritizing it.** It is important that our efforts to end oppression for some do not perpetuate oppression of others.

Remember, while embracing intersectionality is vital for our efforts of fighting racism and other oppression, it applies to all aspects of our lives, not just our movements. Who gets to speak at company meetings? Whom do you vote for? How is your child's school curriculum developed? Who is considered when developing environmental policy? Everything we do publicly can be made more inclusive and uplifting with intersectionality, and everything we do can become exclusionary and oppressive without it. Intersectionality, and the recognition and confrontation of our privilege, can make us better people with better lives.

| six |

Is police brutality really about race?

"JUST GOT PULLED OVER FOR DRIVING WHILE BLACK. Here's hoping I get out of it safely"

This was a Tweet I sent out July of 2015, along with a photo of the officer who had pulled me over. I was driving with my two brothers on the freeway, moving with traffic, slightly over the speed limit (the ticket given put me at 1 mph over the speed limit). I watched the motorcycle cop cross three lanes of traffic to pick my vehicle out of the crowd, slowing all traffic to guide me back to the other side of the busy freeway.

As we waited for the officer to walk up to the passenger side window, my brothers and I tried to calm ourselves down. "Just stay calm, don't ask any questions. We'll be okay," my brother Aham repeated in a voice that betrayed his fear, and also his determination to see us all get through this encounter intact. It was then that I sent the alert to friends and family.

The Tweet I sent once we were stopped on the side of the road is similar to what many of my black friends send out these days when they are pulled over. This message is sent out not so much to complain, but to notify friends and family that if something should happen to you in the near future, this was the likely cause. As we've learned, witnesses are the only defense people of color seem to have against police brutality, and often even that isn't enough.

Our encounter with the officer was over quickly, although it felt like an eternity. He was brusque and professional, while we silently sat in fear—watching our hands to make sure they didn't betray us with any sudden movements, any threatening gestures. Aham's hands shook as he opened my glove compartment to get my vehicle registration, slowly and clearly telling the officer "I'm reaching into the glove compartment now" and waiting for the officer's nod before moving.

Watching my brother carefully reach for the glove compartment I was reminded of one time when I was pulled over at sixteen; I quickly reached for the glove compartment when asked for license and registration and the officer's hand immediately went to his gun as he yelled "STOP!" As I sat there frozen in fear, he proceeded to lecture me to never reach for anything in front of a cop without saying what I was doing first. "That's a good way to get yourself shot, young lady," he said to me. Then he nodded and took his hand off of his gun, satisfied with the favor he had done me by not shooting a sixteen-year-old girl for reaching for her identification.

But this officer did not shout or reach for his gun. He simply wrote out my ticket and then drove off. When the officer was gone, we sat for a moment and collected ourselves. We looked at each other, grateful that we were all okay. I sent out a quick Tweet letting everyone know that we were okay, and then I started driving again, dreading the rest of the long trip that moments earlier we had been looking forward to and driving slowly enough to anger everyone else on the road.

When I got home, I had dozens of messages waiting for me from friends and community members, voicing concern at my first Tweet and relief at my second. Many of those messages came from other black people, who related to the fear behind my initial Tweet and shared their own stories of their DWBs. But there were plenty of other messages from people wondering why I had brought race into it at all.

"Why do you assume it's about race?"

"You have no proof it was anything other than a traffic stop."

"Wouldn't it be better to just assume good intentions on behalf of the cop?"

"How do you know it's about race?"

And the truth is, I didn't know it was about race, and I still don't. There's a very good chance that I just won that horrible lottery and my car, with three black individuals, was the one car to be pulled over out of pure luck. Maybe we're all just really unlucky, as a race.

And while I may have been pulled over due to luck of the draw, the thing is—I can't ask why. The last time my brother asked a cop why he'd been pulled over, the cop leaned into the vehicle and asked ominously, "Are we going to have a problem here?" So he doesn't ask anymore, and after seeing what happened to Sandra Bland, I certainly don't ask either.

If we don't know if each individual encounter with police officers is truly about race, and if we can't safely ask—why do we talk about police brutality like it is about race? At its core, police brutality is about power and corruption. Police brutality is about the intersection of fear and guns. Police brutality is about accountability. And the power and corruption that enable police brutality put *all* citizens, of every race, at risk. But it does not put us at risk equally, and the numbers bear that out. My fear, as a black driver, is real. The fact is that black drivers are 23 percent more likely to be pulled over than white drivers[1], between 1.5 and 5 times more likely to be searched (while shown to be less likely than whites to turn up contraband in these searches),[2] and more likely to be ticketed[3] and arrested[4] in those stops. This increase in stops, searches, and arrests also leads to a 3.5–4 times higher probability that black people will be killed by cops (this increase is the same for Native Americans interacting with police, a shamefully underreported statistic). Even when we aren't arrested or killed, we are still more likely to be abused and dehumanized in our stops. A 2016 review of a thirteen-month period showed that Oakland police handcuffed 1,466 black people in nonarrest traffic stops, and only 72 white people[5], and a 2016 study by the Center for Policing Equity found that blacks were almost 4 times more likely to be subject to force from police—including force by hand (such as hitting and choking), pepper spray, tazer, and gun—than white people.[6]

So maybe that time I got pulled over wasn't about race. Maybe the time I'd been pulled over before that wasn't about race. Maybe even the time before that. But those who demand the smoking gun of a racial slur or swastika or burning cross before they will believe that an individual encounter with the police might be about race are ignoring what we know and what the numbers are bearing out: something is going on and it is not right. We are being targeted. And you can try to explain away one statistic due to geography, one away due to income—you can find reasons for numbers all day. But the fact remains: all across the country, in every type of neighborhood, people of color are being disproportionately criminalized. This is not all in our heads.

When we first learn to drive it's with the same excitement of anybody else newly behind the wheel. A bit of fear mixed with a sense of freedom and power. But while our white friends quickly settle into the mundanity of the daily commute, we never get that sense of ease. The first time I was pulled over was at age sixteen, for going five miles over the speed limit in a wealthy white neighborhood. I explained that I hadn't realized the speed limit had been recently lowered. But the cop wanted to know if I was drunk. If I was on drugs. What he would find if he looked in my trunk (I believe I answered "snacks"). A few months later I was pulled over for not coming to a "complete stop" on a suburban road, empty of all traffic except for me and the officer. I've been stopped for having my vehicle tabs expired by one day (even though it was still within the month indicated on the tab, which meant that the officer was scanning my plates for the hell of it). Time and time again the questions I was asked were along the same lines: "What are you doing in this neighborhood?" "Have you been drinking?" "Do I smell marijuana?" "Do you have any illegal substances or weapons in your car?" I know it sounds silly, but it surprised me every time. I've never been a big drinker; I've never driven drunk, and weed never did anything for me. I have no criminal record, no past indication of dangerous driving or violence. And yet, by the age of eighteen I couldn't shake the feeling that cops were out to get me. And this experience is even worse for many black men and for those who do have criminal records that give cops even more reason to harass them.

Like myself, most people of color I know do not enjoy driving. We have moments where we forget what our blackness means behind the wheel, when we are enjoying a great song on the radio, or leaving a fun event. For a few moments, we are driving like any other carefree American. But then our pulses rise at the sight of an officer on the street. Will this be the time? The moment the lights on the police cruiser go on we know—that's for us. We are watching our speed and using our turn signals and yet when those lights go on we know that there is no other car that officer is going to pull up behind than ours. And we pray that our paperwork is all legit, and that the officer won't be afraid of us, that we won't make the wrong moves or say the wrong things. We hope that all we get out of this encounter is a ticket and a nervous stomach.

And I'm not sure what's worse, the fear and anxiety and fatigue brought on by yet another encounter with an officer that you are hoping and praying to make it out of intact, or the never-ending denial by the rest of society of the fear and anxiety and fatigue you experience as a valid response to the near-constant reminder that those assigned and empowered to protect you see your skin color as evidence of wrongdoing, and could take your freedom or even your life at any time, with no recourse.

In this individualist nation we like to believe that systemic racism doesn't exist. We like to believe that if there are racist cops, they are individual bad eggs acting on their own. And with this belief, we are forced to prove that each individual encounter with the police is definitively racist or it is tossed out completely as mere coincidence. And so, instead of a system imbued with the racism and oppression of greater society, instead of a system plagued by unchecked implicit bias, inadequate training, lack of accountability, racist quotas, cultural insensitivity, lack of diversity, and lack of transparency—we are told we have a collection of individuals doing their best to serve and protect outside of a few bad apples acting completely on their own, and there's nothing we can do about it other than address those bad apples once it's been thoroughly proven that the officer in question is indeed a bad apple.

So, acknowledging us, believing us, means challenging everything you believe about race in this country. And I know that this is a very big ask, I know that this is a painful and scary process. I know that it's hard to believe that the people you look to for safety and security are the same people who are causing us so much harm. But I'm not lying and I'm not delusional. I am scared and I am hurting and we are dying. And I really, really need you to believe me.

FEW SUBJECTS SHED GREATER LIGHT ON THE RACIAL DI-vide in the US than the subject of police brutality. Gallup's polls of white and black Americans on their opinions of police in the US show that more than double the percentage of whites versus blacks have confidence in police or view them as honest and ethical, and whites are twice as likely as blacks to believe that police treat racial minorities fairly.[7]

But this same racial disparity in our feelings about the police is matched by disparities in our encounters with police. As described earlier in this chapter, people of color are more likely to be stopped by police, arrested by police, assaulted by police, and killed by police.

When we look at the difference in opinion towards and confidence in our police force, along with the difference in experiences with our police force, it's easy to wonder how it's possible that we all live in the same country.

If we want to understand how experiences and sentiment between police and communities of different races could be so different, we must first understand the historical relation-ship between police forces and communities of color.

There has not been a time in American history where our police force has not had a contentious and often violent re-lationship with communities of color. Our police forces were born from Night Patrols, who had the principal task of con-trolling black and Native American populations in New En-gland, and Slave Patrols, who had the principal task of catching escaped black slaves and sending them back to slave masters.[8] After the Fugitive Slave Act was passed, catching and reenslav-ing black people became the job of Night Patrols as well, and that job was continued on after the Night Patrols were turned

into the country's first police forces. Our early American police forces existed not only to combat crime, but also to return
black Americans to slavery and control and intimidate free
black populations. Police were rightfully feared and loathed
by black Americans in the North and South.

In the brutal and bloody horror of the post-Reconstruction
South, local police sometimes joined in on the terrorizing of
black communities that left thousands of black Americans
dead.[9] In the South, through the Jim Crow era and the civil
rights movement, it was well known locally that many police
officers were also members of the Ku Klux Klan. Through
much of the eighteenth, nineteenth, and early twentieth centuries, American police forces were one of the greatest threats
to the safety of black Americans.

Our police force was not created to serve black Americans; it was created to police black Americans and serve white
Americans. This is why even when police were donning white
hoods and riding out at night to burn crosses on the lawns
of black families, white families could still look at them with
respect and trust. Our police forces had starkly different roles
within the white community that they were responsible to.

Police abuse and oppression of people of color has not
stopped at black Americans. Hispanic and Native American
populations have also long been the recipients of higher rates
of arrest, assault, and death at the hands of police, and police
have been used throughout history to intimidate, punish, and
silence activists and protestors in all minority racial and ethnic
groups.

Our police forces were created not to protect Americans of
color, but to control Americans of color. People of color were

seen by the police as an inconvenience at best, and a threat at worst, but never as people to protect and serve. This desire to control the behavior of people of color along with disregard for the lives of people of color has been woven throughout the history of American policing. This general attitude toward communities of color was also built into police training and police culture, and strong remnants of that remain today.

It is understandable then that the fear and mistrust of police are also woven throughout the history of communities of color, especially black America. The trauma from police brutality has been felt over multiple generations. The generational wounds of police brutality and oppression have not healed, because the brutality and oppression is still happening, even if cops are no longer wearing white hoods or letting their attack dogs loose on us.

Yes, our police officers are far less likely to be seen joining lynch mobs, and far fewer of them explicitly see "controlling the black population" as their main job. But our police force is much larger and much more powerful than it was in the past, and the narratives and organizational structure that promoted the terrorizing of black Americans and communities of color in the past protects the harassment and brutality against black Americans and communities of color in the present.

This is not to say that the majority of our police officers are racist, hateful monsters. When looking at anti-black bias in police actions, we are looking at the product of police cultural history that has always viewed black Americans as adversaries, and of a popular culture that has always portrayed black Americans as violent criminals not worthy of protection. From our books, TV shows, and movies, to our crime focus on news programs—the narrative of the black brute is as strong now as it was when *Birth of a Nation* was released to wide acclaim in 1915. We hear this repeated in the language of our TV pundits and our politicians. Who will do something about this inner-city crime? Who will keep our streets safe from these thugs? Who will protect us from these super-predators? The belief that black people still need to be controlled by police is promoted by our politicians and funded by our taxpayers.

This belief that black people and people of color are more dangerous, unpredictable, and violent is not something that I believe most police officers (and other Americans) even know they believe. But they do believe it deep down. This implicit bias against people of color is so insidious that not even people of color are exempt from having it, which is why, yes, even police officers of color can show bias against civilians of color. Implicit bias is the beliefs that sit in the back of your brain and inform your actions without your explicit knowledge. In times of stress, these unexamined beliefs can prove deadly.

And a large portion of police encounters with people of color—or with any people for that matter—are high-stress situations where that implicit bias is more likely to take over at any hint of unpredictability or escalation and flood an officer with irrational fear. When an officer shoots an unarmed black man and says he feared for his life, I believe it. But that fear itself is often racist and unfounded.

I would be remiss if I did not acknowledge that there is higher crime in some cities where larger minority populations live. Yes, black men are more likely to commit a violent offense than white men. No, this is not "black-on-black" or "brown-on-brown" crime. Those terms are 100 percent racist. It's crime. We don't call crime that happens in white communities "white-on-white" crime, even though the majority of crimes against white people are perpetrated by other white people. Crime is a problem within communities. And communities with higher poverty, fewer jobs, and less infrastructure are going to have higher crime, regardless of race. When the average black American has one-thirteenth the net worth and the average Hispanic American has one-tenth the net worth of the average white American,[10] and when the poverty rate among Native Americans is over three times that of whites,[11] it is a strong bet that neighborhoods of color are more likely to be poor neighborhoods with higher crime and that higher-priced neighborhoods with easier access to jobs and more funding for education that lead to less crime would be more likely to be populated by comparatively wealthier white people.

Crime in communities of color is often compounded by the contentious relationship with police. Nobody wants a solution to crime in black communities more than black people do, they are the people most impacted by it. But when you cannot trust the police to protect you, who do you call to report illegal activity? When a crime happens, why would you cooperate with a police force that you do not trust to enforce the law without bias or excessive force?

Police, as an extension of American society, are more likely to view people of color as dangerous, and people of color are more likely to view police as corrupt. This may seem on the surface as a simple miscommunication. Old grudges that just need to be let go. This is often how it is discussed by the media and by our politicians. "If we could only come together, we'd see that we're all good people."

But these simple platitudes ignore the power dynamic at play in people of color's interactions with police. Just about every police officer that a person of color encounters will be armed—not just with a gun, but with the full force of a justice system that has shown just as much bias against people of color as the police have. If someone is going to be harmed or killed in a police encounter, the numbers show that it is most likely going to be the civilian, not the police. When that harm is the result of an unjustified use of force against a civilian of color, most people of color know that the police officer involved will likely face very few consequences, if any. Police officers know this, too. This is known in every encounter with police—every traffic stop, every domestic violence call, every welfare call.

People of color do need and desperately want an effective police force to help keep their communities safe. And in order for a police force to be effective, it has to earn the trust of its people. But to those who only scratch the surface, to those who do not investigate their simplistic opinions about the root cause of crime in inner-cities and the animosity between police forces and communities of color—the answer is simply "more policing." But what we need is different policing. Policing not steeped from root to flower in the need to control people of color.

If you are not a person of color, your relationship with these same officers is likely vastly different. The assumption that police officers would serve and protect the white community has existed as long as the assumption that police officers would control people of color. The long, well-established history of violence toward and oppression of the white community simply does not exist in American policing. This does not mean that white Americans were never subject to abuse by police, not at all. A look at our police force's history of abuse and persecution of the LGBT community is one of many examples that show otherwise. But by and large, even with occasional abuses of white civilians by police, most white Americans are confident that the criminal justice system is still to be trusted. Our police force is integral to white American feelings of safety and security in their communities. They are a valued part of the community. To question the integrity of police is to question the safety of the communities they serve, and that can be very unsettling to many who rely on that feeling of protection for their peace of mind.

But that comfort and security that many white Americans have felt with their police is built on the oppression of people of color by those same police. The police don't just keep white communities safe, they save white communities from the evils of inner-city crime. They are the heroes who keep Compton in Compton and Chicago in Chicago. Without the police, your white community would be just like *those* communities, and it is white America's love of police that separates you from a crime-ridden ghetto. This is not something that all white Americans explicitly think or say, but it is the overwhelming narrative of our culture, our politicians, and our police forces. And that narrative shapes a lot of our conversations around policing and race.

When talking about police brutality, it is important to remember that the police force can be trustworthy public servants to one community, and oppressors to another community—just as we can live in a country that promotes prosperity for some and poverty for others. And this can be the same police force and the same country, without making any of these realities invalid. While numbers show that people of color are disproportionately targeted by police, they also show that white people in general trust and admire police. Both these statistics are true.

But our goal should be to ensure that people of all races are able to feel safe and secure with our police forces. We need to recognize that the fear that people of color have of police is not merely rooted in feeling or culture, but in the separate and violent history that our police forces have with communities of color. We must realize that there are two very different realities of how our police interact with white communities and with communities of color, and both of those realities have their own structure and history. We cannot address police brutality if we are not willing to recognize these differences and address the entirety of the specific history and structure of police interactions with communities of color.

It is important when talking about police brutality to stand secure in your experience, without trying to override the experiences of other communities with police. What has happened to you is valid and true, but it is not what has happened to everyone. The experience of white communities with police are real, and the experience of communities of color with police are real—but they are far from the same. And while it is important to recognize these different viewpoints, we must remember this: If you do trust and value your police force, and you also believe in justice and equality for people of color, you will not see the lack of trust on behalf of communities of color as simply a difference of opinion. You will instead expect your police force to earn the respect and trust of communities of color by providing them with the same level of service that you enjoy. People of color are not asking white people to believe their experiences so that they will fear the police as much as people of color do. They are asking because they want white people to join them in demanding their right to be able to trust the police like white people do.

seven

How can I talk about affirmative action?

"JOMA, IT'S TIME FOR YOU TO STEP OUTSIDE NOW."
I quietly grabbed my pencil and folder and walked out the door while the rest of my first-grade class watched.

In the hallway stood a teacher's aide, next to two tiny desks. In my memory the hallway was dark and foreboding, but I think now that any empty school hallway seems dark and foreboding to a small child regardless of lighting. From a classroom a few doors away, a brown boy exited into the hallway and sat at his desk, and I took a seat in mine. The teacher's aide did not seem like a real teacher to me, she seemed like a big kid. Looking back on it, I think she was probably a college student. She was friendly and cheerful, but I resented her anyway. I didn't like being in this dark hallway, away from my class. I didn't like how much more it set me apart from my peers.

"How's your book report coming, Joma?" she asked, her smile unrecognizing of my seven-year-old anger. I quickly shook off my resentment and launched into excited ramblings about my favorite subject: books.

We had moved to this neighborhood a few months earlier. We couldn't afford our apartment in our old suburb, even without a phone or electricity after both had been shut off due to nonpayment. And even though we had to sneak into the "show" apartment down the hall at night to boil water for ramen and to shower (after a sympathetic manager had given my mom a key), I loved our neighborhood and my school. My teachers were excited by my aptitude and love of learning and had talked with my mom about moving me ahead a grade or putting me in an advanced program.

But even my seven-year-old self could see that my mom was struggling to make ends meet. We had roommates for a while, another single mom and her two young children, and the six of us were doing okay in the three-bedroom apartment. But my mom had come home one day and caught her roommate beating her five-year-old son in the head with a plastic baseball bat, and after the dust settled and the cops had left, it was just the three of us again. And we were no longer able to get by.

When my mom became eligible for family housing near the university she was attending, she jumped at the chance, and we moved to converted army barracks in the city. I said goodbye to my friends and my teachers and started at a new school, in a new neighborhood where I definitely didn't belong. The school that I moved to was very diverse and very poor. Many of the kids in class were also kids who, like us, depended on government assistance for most of our food and the community garden for the rest. Many of the kids seemed older than me—not in physical age, but in life lived. They wandered our neighborhood with a freedom and abandon that I knew my mom would never grant me. They hung out with older siblings and told stories of fights they'd seen, and some they'd even joined in on. I had never seen a fight, except for the seconds I'd seen of my mom's interaction with her roommate months earlier before she told us to go to the neighbor's apartment and wait for her to come get us. I didn't know the jokes, the games, or the slang of these kids. I felt like I'd moved to another country, and not simply another city.

Most of the kids that I remember in my school were latch-key kids, their own responsibility while their parents worked multiple jobs just to get by. I remember the distinct difference in parental involvement in education at that school compared to my old school—in that it just didn't exist at my new school. Parents were too busy trying to put food on the table, and so all educational needs were left, by necessity not choice, to an extremely underfunded school.

My mom had more time than most parents at my school, not because she had more money, but because she was a student and her schedule allowed for an hour or two between classes to volunteer at my class when she could. My mom believed that education was our only way out of the poverty we knew and had spent the last twelve years working toward her bachelor's degree whenever she could scrape together enough money, loans, and time to attend classes. She pestered my new teachers into doing whatever they could to nurture the talent I showed. And so, a few times a week, I was sent to the hallway to read and write with the other kid identified as "gifted." This was the best they could do.

My brother Aham, a very talented kid in his own right, did not fare so well. His emotionality and energy had been misinterpreted in the same way it is for many young black boys—as aggression and lack of intelligence. One teacher, who had given up on my brother altogether, told my mom that she thought Aham had "cotton between his ears." When the school refused to move her son to a different classroom, my mom became a regular volunteer in the class, sitting in the back of the room and staring at the teacher, to ensure that she treated my brother with at least feigned kindness.

As the years went by and we moved from neighborhood to neighborhood and school to school, as financial woes drove us out with each rent increase, my school record followed. My quiet demeanor and love of books had me singled out as "different" from the other black kids and each teacher treated me as a sort of unicorn, trying to preserve what they saw in me as "rare." For my brother, his reputation as a troubled black boy also followed him from school to school and class to class.

One day, in fifth grade, two girls I knew from my brother's class ran up to me.

"Your brother's homeless!" they shouted, giggling, before running away again.

I had no idea what they were talking about, but I quickly forgot the exchange altogether.

A few days later, we were heading to assembly in the school gymnasium when my class line crossed paths with Aham's class line.

"Hi!" Aham eagerly shouted at me and I raised my hand and waved.

"Homeless! Homeless!" a few kids shouted at him and my brother's face clouded in shame. He blinked back tears. Before I could say anything, they had passed me by.

After a few days, I was able to get a girl in Aham's class to explain what was happening. Their teacher had set up a unique system of reward and punishment in the classroom. She had printed out fake money for the class and gave them each a few dollars to start. If you were attentive in class, you were given money. If you turned your homework in, you got money, and so on. And if you spoke out of turn, you lost money. If you forgot your homework, you lost money. If your desk was messy, you lost money. If, at the end of the week, you had leftover money, you could use it to buy treats or stickers or other small gifts. But there was a catch.

You had to pay rent first. On your desk.

My brother had already been singled out as a difficult kid, and the teacher was taking money from him before he could make it. And his upset over losing money would cause him to act out and lose more. So while every Friday students would eagerly line up to pick out their piece of candy, my brother would sit.

On the floor. Because he was homeless. He couldn't afford rent on his desk.

The days spread to weeks and the weeks spread to months and my brother became known as "the homeless kid." It was a taunt that followed him everywhere, eating into his soul. I do not think that his teacher knew that we had, in fact, been actually homeless at times. But how she could miss the impact that this new homelessness was having upon a little boy, I'll never know. By the end of the year, my energetic, sensitive brother became permanently sad and anxious. He didn't make a single friend for years.

My brother and I went on our separate paths through the rest of our school years. I went on to take early college courses. Aham dropped out of high school, his daily panic attacks making social interaction impossible, and we could not afford to get him help. The only thing that kept my brother alive was music. And after he dropped out of high school and the pre-judgment of teachers was gone, Aham was easily able to pass his test for his GED. And he then successfully interviewed for and received a scholarship to music school. Without music, he would have been lost.

I got married at twenty and had my firstborn son, Malcolm, shortly after. But the marriage was unhealthy and at times abusive, and I had to get out. By the time I was twenty-two, I was a single parent. I had never forgotten my mom's dedication to education. After a few years of struggling in entry-level customer service work, knowing that I only had one option to escape the poverty that she'd had to raise us in, I moved my son and me ninety miles away, and went to college.

I had no family money to help pay for college, but the early nurturing of my teachers had left me with a strong enough academic record for admission, and outside of a few grants, I was able to pay for the bulk of my tuition in loans that I was not sure that I'd ever be able to pay back.

Over the next few years I fought my way to a degree, enduring many a sleepless night as I balanced school, work, and being the sole caretaker of a young boy. I remember feeling so tired, and so alone. I remember looking at my student loan balance with dread, and looking with jealousy and resentment at my classmates whose parents had at least been able to offer some help. I remember wishing that I, too, could crash for a few days after finals week, instead of waking up the next morning to take my son to the bus. I was always the only black person in my classes, and my entire time in the university I only encountered one black professor. I was constantly translating my opinions to a class that did not understand the political viewpoints of a black woman who had lived a life they would never know. I remember having no friends. I also remember knowing that I couldn't fuck up. Not once. I couldn't change my major, couldn't fail a class. But I loved school, and despite the challenges, I flourished in college in my own solitary way, just as I had in elementary school. And in 2007 I received my bachelor's degree, the day after my son graduated from kindergarten.

After graduation, I was engaged to be married and pregnant with my second child. I quickly found work, from a college referral program, with a telecom company. The work had less than nothing to do with my degree in political science, but it was a job, and because I had a degree—any degree—and because the college referral program set me up with phone interviews where nobody could see my black skin and pregnant belly, I was able to ask for a living wage.

I was, at twenty-five, still the same child who had been told every day that she was different and special. Knowing that, I dove into my new career with gusto. I volunteered for special projects, worked unpaid overtime to learn new skills, found new ways to save the company money. I applied for a promotion and interviewed well. A manager came by my desk one day, "Congratulations," he said, "They announced it in the manager's meeting today. You're moving on to better things." I was ecstatic, this was my first promotion. Word quickly spread as another manager stopped by my desk to loudly congratulate me, and while some people were happy for me, others were not.

The next day I was pulled into my manager's office. He looked pained.

"There's been some rumor that you've gotten the promotion you applied for. I apologize for any mention of that getting to you, because unfortunately it's not true. I don't know how this misinformation got to you, but I'm sorry."

"I was told by two separate managers that they'd been told by you," I said, tears welling up in my eyes.

"That's simply not true," replied my manager and reiterated, "I'm sorry. You're talented and your time will come."

I had been lied to. Something had happened to my promotion, but there was nothing I could do. I was crushed for a few days, but I recovered and kept working. A few months later, another opening came up in the department I had interviewed for earlier. I interviewed and was formally offered the position.

When I arrived at the new department, I was told by a teammate that they'd all expected me sooner, but when word of my first supposed promotion got out, a white woman who had also applied complained and said that because I hadn't been at the company as long as she had, it was obvious that I had been promoted because I was black. She had threatened to sue, so the promotion went to her instead.

That insinuation that I'd been promoted because of my skin color stuck, even though I was one of only about five people of color in my entire department. I had the highest stats, stayed late almost every night even though I had two kids at home, and took on any extra projects available to me. And yet, the grumbling and rumors persisted: I didn't deserve any of my accolades or promotions. Along with the resentment of my race, there was the sexual harassment that came from being a woman in a primarily male department. I'd be asked to split a lunch only to find out that I'd somehow agreed to a date. Unwanted gifts were left on my desk. Suggestive "jokes" were made about my body. I remember one senior engineer leaning over my desk to tell me how many women he'd slept with over the years, then he paused and looked at my pregnant belly and asked, "So, are you going to deliver vaginally?"

Even with the unpleasant environment, I still did better than other people of color in the department. My teammate Terrence, who had trained me when I was first promoted onto the team, had been with the company about three years longer than I had. He was a hard-working black man, with a wife and three kids at home. One day I showed up to work and his usually cheerful demeanor was gone. In fact, he looked like he was going to have to cry. During break, I asked him what was wrong.

"Between you and me, I think I'm going to have to quit," he said.

He explained that he had been offered another job at a rival company. He didn't want to leave, but his family really needed the increase in pay that had been offered. He had told our manager about his predicament, and our manager and director had agreed to match the hourly wage that the competitor had offered. Terrence turned down the job with the competitor, happy to stay at the company that he'd been with for years.

But that morning, our director and manager had sat him down and said that they were not, in fact, able to give him the raise they had promised. They said that because he didn't have a college degree, Terrence was not eligible for that pay level, and it had not been approved by senior management. He was offered an increase of $1 an hour instead of the $5 an hour promised in the offer he'd just declined.

When Terrence told me how much he was currently making and what was offered, I was aghast. Even with the raise, it was less than I had made on my first day of work at the company, and even further behind what other team members made, all except for a Latinx mother of five, who we discovered was making even less than Terrence—barely over minimum wage for the complex technical work we did.

I left that company shortly after. I could not work at a place that I didn't trust, a place where employees of color felt exploited and unappreciated, and I was lucky to have options with other companies. On my last day, I sat with an HR manager for my exit interview. One of the first questions she asked me was, "Do you think you deserved your promotions?" After I left that interview, a manager from a neighboring team came up to me and asked, plainly and without shame, "Are you leaving because of all of the times that I sexually harassed you?"

My next job was at a much more progressive company, but still, my identity as a black woman was always an issue. In five years, I only worked for one manager of color. When I was promoted out of that team, the first thing my new white boss did was ask if my hair was real. While my work was respected, socially I struggled. The "bright" and "energetic" reputation that I had always had was soon augmented with "loud" and "opinionated." One teammate came up to me and said, "I'm surprised how much I like you, I'd heard you were a really strong woman."

I wasn't the only black person who had somehow been labeled overly aggressive at the office, as was hinted at the few times when I was alone with the handful of other black people in my division. The company started an annual employee satisfaction survey and every year senior management would gather us all together and go over the results. The surveys were a big deal, with reminders going out daily until there was as close to a 100 percent completion rate as possible. A few of the questions had to do with the company's diversity efforts. Something like, do people of color feel like they have equal opportunity with their peers? The survey results read a pretty resounding "no."

In our meeting to discuss the survey, all the other questions had been delved into with talk of how the company was working to either address lagging performance, or further encourage strong performance. But not when this question showed up on the projector. The director presenting the results paused after reading the question and said, "I'm pretty sure that people just didn't understand the question." She then shrugged and added, "I'm sure that next year's results would show that." She continued on to the next slide.

I heard a black man next to me grumble, "I sure understood the question."

As I fought for promotions, I quickly found myself alone: the only black woman in my division. I was lonely and disheartened, but I kept working hard to try to make enough money to take care of my family.

I started writing to escape that loneliness, to reach a community outside of my office. And I was lucky to discover that the little girl who had loved words was still inside me. I was a good writer. I was also lucky that I started writing at a time when society was starting to pay more attention to issues of race. Whereas, in the office, my thoughts on race and society in America would have made me a pariah, they were welcomed in the online publishing world. Social media had broken down traditional publishing barriers as readers clamored for authentic voices on important social issues. Suddenly, publishers usually helmed by white men, used to publishing mostly white men, were scouring the Internet for voices of black people, brown people, women, and queer folk. But I quickly discovered that while the publishing opportunity had increased in recent years, the ability to make any money at it had decreased. And while bylines diversified, the publishers did not. So while a writer of color may be asked to write 700 words about Beyoncé for a nominal commission, the staff writing and editing jobs—with their regular salaries and health benefits—stayed with white men.

How can I talk about affirmative action?

As I juggled my day job in a hostile environment with the writing that I loved, I wondered if I'd ever be able to write full time. As I watched many female writers of color leave the field after years of not being able to earn a living wage while receiving countless hateful comments by white people threatened by their words, I doubted that dream would ever come true.

You can imagine my shock when I was offered a part-time staff writing job at a new publisher. I had written some pieces for the founders of the publication for other magazines in the past, and they valued my work and wanted my voice. They had enough funding for one year, and would give me enough salary to just barely cover my mortgage, plus health benefits. I jumped at the chance, and quit my day job. And ever since then I've been hustling every day, working for primarily white editors at various publishers whenever something "black" happens in the media that they want my take on, scrambling to get enough freelance work to pay my bills every month. It has been tough, but I've made it work so far. I still don't know where I'll be a year from now, if I'll be able to still call myself a writer. And still every day, I know that I'm one of the lucky ones.

I have found myself now, at thirty-six, with a writing career. For some, who know my history, I'm seen as someone who beat the odds and fought against adversity and won. "You must be so proud," they say.

And I am proud, but mostly, I'm angry. I'm angry, because when I look around, I'm still alone. I'm still the only black woman in the room. And when I look at what I've fought so hard to accomplish next to those who will never know that struggle I wonder, "How many were left behind?" I think about my first-grade class and wonder how many black and brown kids weren't identified as "talented" because their parents were too busy trying to pay bills to pester the school the way my mom did. Surely there were more than two, me and the brown boy who sat next to me in the hall each day. I think about my brother and wonder how many black boys were similarly labeled as "trouble" and were unable to claw out of the dark abyss that my brother had spent so many years in. I think about the boys and girls playing at recess who were dragged to the principal's office because their dark skin made their play look like fight. I think about my friend who became disillusioned with a budding teaching career, when she worked at the alternative school and found that it was almost entirely populated with black and brown kids who had been sent away from the general school population for minor infractions. From there would only be expulsions or juvenile detention.

I think about every black and brown person, every queer person, every disabled person, who could be in the room with me, but isn't, and I'm not proud. I'm heartbroken. We should not have a society where the value of marginalized people is determined by how well they can scale often impossible obstacles that others will never know. I have been exceptional, and I shouldn't have to be exceptional to be just barely getting by. But we live in a society where if you are a person of color, a disabled person, a single mother, or an LGBT person you have to be exceptional. And if you are exceptional by the standards put forth by white supremacist patriarchy, and you are lucky, you will most likely just barely get by. There's nothing inspirational about that.

"AFFIRMATIVE ACTION" IS A TERM THROWN AROUND wildly in conversations about race—usually by those who are firmly on the "there is no racism/there is only reverse-racism/affirmative action is racist against white people" crowd. When not used as an argument, it's used as an insult: "Oh yeah, you're just an affirmative action hire." But for all the talk—for all those who tear it down and all those who try to defend it—not many people fully understand affirmative action.

I mean, we sort of get the concept. Affirmative action is supposed to combat bias in work and education by mandating a certain amount of hires and admissions from minority groups. It is supposed to force a more level playing field. But it's in our ignorance of the details that we lose the entire plot.

First introduced by President Kennedy and expanded by President Johnson in the '60s, affirmative action sought to help reverse extreme racial gaps in federal employment and higher education. The intention was to get federal employers to proactively fight racial discrimination in their hiring practices and to increase the African American undergraduate population above its then dismal 5 percent. Shortly after its introduction, affirmative action was expanded to all women.

Affirmative action took many forms throughout the US. At colleges and universities, it often took the form of increased recruitment efforts, extra consideration given to race and gender in the selection process, academic support programs, and increased financial aid. In federal employment, it often took similar forms—increased recruitment efforts, extra consideration given to race and gender, and diversity goals. There were no "quotas," and any attempts at such were struck down by the Supreme Court. Employers and educators could set forth goals to increase diversity, provided there were enough qualified people of color or women to make such goals reasonable. These were never huge percentages and were most often below a representational percentage. For example: when the Supreme Court upheld a 10 percent set-aside of contract funds for minority businesses in 1980, that percentage was far below representative of the 17 percent minority population at the time.[1] Affirmative action's goal was to force educators and federal employers to get creative and proactive in their efforts to combat the effects that hundreds of years of racial and gender discrimination had had on the diversity of their workplaces and universities.

By the time Reagan rolled into office, affirmative action was on the decline as many conservatives declared it no longer necessary. Bit by bit, piece by piece, affirmative action has been chipped away at over the last thirty years, leaving a program that can hardly be called affirmative.

But remnants of affirmative action, especially in our colleges and universities, are still the target of many who believe that affirmative action is unjust. And as affirmative action practices are rolled back in higher education institutions across the country, the enrollment and graduation rates of people of color in many of those institutions are plummeting. Affirmative action is a crucial tool if we want to mitigate some of the effects of systemic racism and misogyny in our society. It should not be rolled back; in fact, I argue that it should be expanded to other groups that suffer from systemic oppression as well. Why? Because it works. No, it doesn't work wonders, but affirmative action can do some good for those who need it, and it can do some good for a society that wants to value equality and diversity.

Believe it or not, conversations around affirmative action can be easier than other conversations around race. Why? Because the majority of the costs and benefits of affirmative action are easily supported by data, and the arguments against it are easily countered. Let's take a look at some of the arguments against affirmative action, and some of the ways in which we can use those arguments to further understanding of why affirmative action is still very necessary.

Argument 1: We don't need affirmative action because society isn't as racist or sexist as it used to be. While racism and sexism can be hard to quantify and compare (we can't exactly call people up and say "how racist are you today"), we can easily see the effects of systemic racism and sexism and oppression in our society today—particularly in our employment and education sectors. Studies have shown that if you have a "black-sounding" name, you are four times less likely to be called for a job interview. White women still make only 82 cents for every white man's dollar, black women only earn 65 cents for every white man's dollar, and Hispanic women earn even less at 58 cents for every white man's dollar. The wage gap between white and black men has not budged since Reagan's cuts to affirmative action began in the '80s, with black men making 73 cents for every white man's dollar, and the wage gap between white and Hispanic men has actually grown since 1980, going from 71 cents down to 69 cents for every dollar made by a white man.[2]

In education, students of color are disadvantaged their entire school career. Black and Hispanic students are far more likely to be suspended from school, starting as early as preschool. An average of 16 percent of black students and 7 percent of Hispanic students are suspended each year, compared to only 5 percent of white students. And while the rate of suspension for white students has remained steady for over thirty years, the rate of suspension for black students has almost tripled.[3] How does this happen? There are a lot of factors, but a Yale study shows that preschool teachers are more likely to look for problem behavior in black children, expect it in black children, and empathize less with children of a different race than their own.[4] Another study of secondary school teachers found that teachers were more likely to call parents of children of color to report problem behavior than they were to call parents of white children, and they were less likely to call parents of children of color to report positive accomplishments than they were to call white parents.[5] When you add this bias to the fact that children of color are more susceptible to food insecurity; are more likely to have to work after school; are less likely to have financial resources to supply regular Internet, study guides, and tutoring; and are more likely to attend underfunded schools—children of color get to their college applications at a stark disadvantage. And this shows in the numbers. Currently, black and Hispanic students are underrepresented in the vast majority of colleges and universities, by 20 percent. A study by the University of Washington shows that enrollment of minority students drops

23 percent when schools enact an affirmative action ban.[6] Only two colleges in the US with affirmative action bans have representational enrollment of black students, and only one has representational enrollment of Hispanic students.[7]

Argument 2: If an employer is racist or sexist, you can just sue them. Here's the thing, an employer can make up just about any excuse for why they did not hire someone, did not promote someone, or fired someone. Unless you can prove malice, unless there is a paper trail of racism or sexism, it is incredibly hard to get a judge to find in your favor. In "no fault" states, an employer can fire an employee for just about any reason and it is the responsibility of the employee to prove discrimination. Furthermore, when most employers demand confidentiality about salary, it's hard for employees to even know that they are being discriminated against in their wages. But when we see far fewer women and people of color being interviewed, hired, and promoted in certain fields, we know that there is a problem that needs to be addressed.

Argument 3: Affirmative action teaches people of color and women that they don't have to work as hard as white men. Sigh. Here's the basic truth: the vast majority of affirmative action goals aim for a representative number of people of color and women. This means that if there are 10 percent black people in the area, the ultimate goal (not quota) would be around 10 percent black employees or students. The goal is simply equal opportunity for female applicants and applicants of color. Why would a representational number of people of color be so much less competitive than a representational number of white people? Is it really only direct competition with white men that motivates women and people of color to work hard?

Argument 4: Affirmative action is unfair to white men because it causes them to lose opportunities to less qualified women and people of color. As with argument 3, remember that these are representational goals, of which we are falling far short. When you say that a representational number of women or people of color cuts out more deserving white men, you are saying that women and people of color deserve to be less represented in our schools and our companies and that white men are deserving of an over-representational majority of these spots. We see the disparities in jobs and education among race and gender lines. Either you believe these disparities exist because you believe that people of color and women are less intelligent, less hard working, and less talented than white men, or you believe that there are systemic issues keeping women and people of color from being hired into jobs, promoted, paid a fair wage, and accepted into college.

Argument 5: Affirmative action doesn't work. This is not true. While affirmative action may not have been the racial panacea that some had originally hoped, it has been one of the most successful programs for helping combat the end-effects of racial discrimination in education and employment that we've tried. Multiple studies have shown that affirmative action programs increased the percentage of people of color in jobs in the public sector and drastically increased the number of people of color in colleges and universities. And while the arguments around affirmative action often come down to race, white women have been by far the biggest recipients of the benefits of affirmative action.

Yes, affirmative action, when fully implemented, can make a measurably positive impact on the socioeconomic outlook for women and people of color who are in the position to benefit from it. Is it the final answer we've been waiting for to end racial oppression? Absolutely not. In truth, even if implemented across the public and private sectors, even if vigorously enforced, affirmative action will never be more than a Band-Aid on a festering sore as long as it's still just trying to correct the end effects of systemic racism. If there is some critique of affirmative action that I'm inclined to agree with it is those posed by academics like Michelle Alexander in *The New Jim Crow*. The argument against affirmative action that holds the most water for me is that when affirmative action is viewed as "enough" it can be detrimental to the fight for racial justice. We must never forget that without systemic change and without efforts to battle the myriad of ways in which systemic racism impacts people of color of all classes, backgrounds, and abilities, our efforts at ending systemic racial oppression will fail. We must refuse to be placated by measures that only serve a select few—and affirmative action does only serve a select few. We must never forget that people of color who will never want to go to college, who will never be able to go to college, who cannot work, who choose not to work, who choose to work in the public sector—they all deserve to be treated as human beings free from racial bigotry and persecution. We must remember that there are other, huge crises affecting communities of color that also need to be addressed with urgency (like the mass incarceration of black and Hispanic men in America). But the work to truly end systemic racism, while crucial, is a long and hard road. And while we are fighting that battle, many people of color are being crushed by a racist educational and employment system and their children are inheriting that same disadvantage as they try to enter into higher education and the workforce. Affirmative action can help with that. Even if we were to flip a switch today and end all racism and racial oppression, millions of people of color would still be disadvantaged by racial oppression of yesterday, and that would need to be addressed with policies like affirmative action that seek to replace opportunities previously denied unless we feel like leaving an entire generation in the dust and hope that their children will be able to rise from those ashes.

We have to fight for our future, we have to work for change, but we also need to help people now.

eight

What is the school-to-prison pipeline?

ACCORDING TO THE LETTER FROM HIS SCHOOL THAT his mom forwarded to me, Sagan was having a very bad day. He had pushed one teacher, struck two others. He had refused to listen to instructions and he refused to stay in his classroom. He was mimicking a gun with his hand and pointing it at students. Sagan had assaulted teachers and threatened students and would be suspended from school. A school board member was arguing that charges should be filed against him.

"Her son assaulted two staff members," the email said. The staff member documenting the incidents also noted that Sagan's mom, Natasha, was not apparently interested in discussing the matter with him at the moment. It really seemed like she just couldn't be bothered.

I was reading this letter at first thinking, wow, Sagan really is a threat to his school. Multiple assaults and disruptions, all in one day. A suspension seems, if anything, light. I began questioning why Natasha, whom I had run into on a few previous occasions at community gatherings but did not know very well, had been so dismissive when confronted by school officials with her son's violent behavior.

It wasn't until I got to the bottom of the email, when the school staff member described having Sagan draw what happened that day and they indicated that he had drawn a number "5" on his drawing of himself, that I realized that I had misunderstood what was very wrong indeed—not with Sagan, with the school.

Why was Sagan drawing a "5" on himself? Because he was only five years old.

When I talked to Natasha a few days after the incident, she was still reeling. Her son Sagan, portrayed as a violent, out-of-control kid in the school email, had never been in trouble at school before. But his day had started out poorly, and as the discipline continued with each outburst, he acted out more and more. There's no indication in the many paragraphs documenting the incidents that any staff members tried to redirect Sagan's energy or ask him why he was upset. Each of the four staff members he encountered that day simply ordered him to stop doing what he was doing, and instituted some sort of punishment when he didn't respond the way that they wanted.

When his mom came to pick him up early from school due to a prearranged appointment that the school had already been made aware of, she was being honest when she said that she did not have time to talk with staff right then. When the staffer tried to shock her into staying by blurting out that her son had "assaulted" multiple staff members that day, Natasha was appalled. As a mother, an educator, and a black woman, she was fully aware of what "assaulted" can mean when you are describing the behavior of black boys.

I am the mother of two boys and I remember what five looks like. I know from experience that five-year-olds are just learning self-control and empathy, and the slightest stressor—a coming cold, a missed breakfast, lack of sleep—can turn a five-year-old into a monster. I have been hit by five-year-olds. Many parents and caregivers have. It is not okay, and there are consequences—usually a time-out followed with a long discussion. But it is not assault. Why? Because I'm a thirty-six-year-old adult who is not going to be irreparably harmed by the blows of someone barely out of toddlerdom, and because I understand that young children are . . . well . . . young children.

Nobody asked if Sagan was feeling well, nobody asked if Sagan was frustrated or sad or uncomfortable about something. Nobody took the time to figure out how they could help this boy (the only black boy in his entire class), nobody asked what they could do to help Sagan rejoin his class and be able to learn alongside his fellow classmates.

He was simply suspended. He was denied education. Five months into his kindergarten year and Sagan had already learned that his teachers did not want him in class, that he was too "bad" to be educated. Luckily for Sagan and his mother, they did not follow up on the school board member's recommendation and press charges against the five-year-old for "threatening" students with his finger gun. Natasha was eventually able to convince the school to lift Sagan's suspension, after pleading, arguing, and threatening to sue. She is still not sure how she is going to get Sagan to love school again. But at least she was able to keep the system from swallowing her son completely, for now.

OUR PUBLIC-SCHOOL SYSTEM SEES BLACK AND BROWN children as violent, disruptive, unpredictable future criminals.

This may seem like the hyperbole of an angry black woman, but when I look at the way in which our black and brown students are treated in schools, it is the only conclusion I can come to.

Black students make up only 16 percent of our school populations, and yet 31 percent of students who are suspended and 40 percent of students who are expelled are black. Black students are 3.5 times more likely to be suspended than white students. Seventy percent of students who are arrested in school and referred to law enforcement are black. In the 2011–2012 school year alone, 92,000 students were arrested.[1]

When I look at these numbers, there are two possible explanations. I can assume that our black and brown children *are* violent, disruptive, unpredictable future criminals who are not deserving of the same access to education as white children. I can assume that there is something fundamentally wrong with black and brown people, something fundamentally broken that is sending our kids out of school and into prison.

Or, I can assume that the school system is marginalizing, criminalizing, and otherwise failing our black and brown kids in large numbers.

I am a black woman, who was at one time a black child, who is raising brown children, who has known and loved countless other black and brown children, who believes that children of any color are amazing gifts of unimaginable possibility to be cherished and protected. I know that we are not broken.

So the only conclusion I can come to is the same conclusion that numerous scholars, activists, even educators have come to: we have a serious problem with how our schools are educating and disciplining black and brown children. And that problem is called the school-to-prison pipeline.

The "school-to-prison pipeline" is the term commonly used to describe the alarming number of black and brown children who are funneled directly and indirectly from our schools into our prison industrial complex, contributing to devastating levels of mass incarceration that lead to one in three black men and one in six Latino men going to prison in their lifetimes, in addition to increased levels of incarceration for women of color.

The school-to-prison pipeline starts with the high level of suspensions and expulsions mentioned earlier. The disproportionately punitive levels of school discipline toward black and brown children does more than impact a student's year. Psychologists attest that overly harsh discipline destroys children's trust in teachers and schools, along with damaging their self-esteem.[2] Students suspended from school are more likely to have to repeat that entire year, or they may choose to drop out entirely. Students arrested at school are more likely to be arrested again in the future. Young boys whose fathers have served jail time are more likely to be deemed emotionally "unready" for school, repeating the cycle of trouble and disproportionate discipline in their classrooms.[3]

Those of you in the educational fields, or who know and love educators, may wonder if I'm insinuating that teachers who have dedicated their lives to educating our children are actually evil racists who hate black and brown children and are working to destroy them. I have known and appreciated many amazing teachers—some who made a positive impact on my life, some who've made positive impacts on the lives of my children. I am very aware that teachers are underpaid, underappreciated, overworked, and often overwhelmed. When we look at the school-to-prison pipeline we must understand that while many teachers do contribute to the problems that black and brown children face, there are many other contributing factors to the disenfranchisement and criminalization of our youth in schools.

So what factors do contribute to the school-to-prison pipeline? Here are some main contributors:

- **Racial bias of school administrators.** Our school employees are not exempt from the racist influences of our society. The image of violent black and brown youth impacts us all and it makes its way into school policy. Studies have indicated that race is really a deciding factor of how and whether students are disciplined. The punitive level of school discipline—how harshly children are punished—is positively correlated with how many black children are in a school, not with, what many would expect, the level of drug or delinquency problems at a school.[4]

- **Racial bias of teachers.** As discussed previously in this book, studies have shown that teachers are more likely to look for trouble in black and brown children and to view the play of black and brown children as aggression.
- **Lack of cultural sensitivity for black and brown children.** Many teachers are unprepared to deal with the challenges that black and brown children are more likely to face—children who are more likely be arriving at school already disadvantaged due to the poverty and insecurity facing many families of color. The vast majority of teachers are white females, and many are unfamiliar with and not trained to work with the different ways in which black and brown children—especially black and brown boys—can interact with each other and with adults. This lack of teacher communication skills, understanding, and resources in working with black and brown children may help explain why black children are more likely to be suspended for subjective reasons, like being "disrespectful" to a teacher, while white children are more likely to be suspended for provable reasons, like drugs or violence.[5]
- **The pathologizing of black children.** Many (likely underfunded and understaffed) schools who find themselves ill-equipped to work with black students who are having interpersonal issues in class are quicker to give students a blanket diagnosis of learning disability than they would with struggling white students. This segregates black children from the general population of white students, abandoning them to our already strained and underperforming special education programs that are

not designed to meet the needs of kids who do not have developmental disabilities or true learning disabilities, but are simply a disciplinary challenge. While black children are no more likely than children of other races to have developmental or learning disabilities, they are the most likely to be placed in special education programs. Students of color who have been labeled "disabled" are more likely (by 31 percent) to be suspended and expelled from school than other kids, a harmful marriage of both ableism and racism. One in four black, American Indian, Pacific Islander, and mixed-race boys identified by schools as having a developmental disability was suspended in the 2011–2012 school year.[6]

- **Zero-tolerance policies.** Fear of violent black and brown youth, compounded by high-profile school shootings primarily perpetrated by white youth, led to the rise of zero-tolerance policies in schools beginning in the '90s. The Gun-Free Schools Act of 1994 mandated a year-long suspension for kids caught bringing a weapon to school. A year-long suspension can be devastating to a child's educational outlook. And as schools have broadly identified "weapons" as anything from guns and knives to camping forks and "finger-guns," black and brown children have found themselves disproportionately affected by these rules and suspended at increasing rates.[7]
- **Increased police presence in schools.** Along with zero-tolerance policies came a rise in the number of police officers in schools, known as School Resource Officers (SROs). These officers have become an easy way for schools to delegate their disciplinary responsibilities to

a criminal justice system that has already shown quantifiable racial bias. Data shows that, when controlling for poverty, schools with SROs have nearly five times the amount of in-school arrests as schools without SROs.

THE SCHOOL-TO-PRISON PIPELINE IS A COMPLEX ISSUE, but it is easy to see that it is vital that we start talking about it more. So how do we address and confront the school-to-prison pipeline in conversation? Here are some tips:

- **Include the school-to-prison pipeline in your broader discussions of racial inequality and oppression.** Far too often, the school-to-prison pipeline is only discussed in academic and activist circles, but it is an issue that touches the lives of countless children of color—and their white friends. It is also deeply interconnected with issues that we do talk about often, like police brutality, mass incarceration, and the wage gap.
- **Talk to your schools and school boards.** Even if you do not have black or brown children, you should be asking your schools what their disciplinary procedures are, what the rate of suspension and expulsion for black and Latinx students is, and what the racial "achievement gap" for their school is and what they plan to do about it. This should be a top priority for all schools, but it only will be if we make it an issue they cannot ignore. (I and many other people of color prefer the term "opportunity gap" as that focuses on the cause of academic disparity shown in grades, graduation rates, and testing

scores—less opportunity for children of color to flourish in education than white children—instead of the end result. This also puts more responsibility for improvement on the education system instead of on the shoulders of disadvantaged children.)

- **Recognize the achievements of black and brown children.** While I believe that exceptionalizing black and brown children (i.e., "Look, here's a good one!") can do more harm than good, the truth is that the everyday achievements of black and brown children are more likely to go unnoticed, while their shortcomings are more likely to be called out. Recognize everyday wins, just as you would white children, not as rare exceptions or as othering "triumph over adversity" stories, but as expected achievements of children just as capable as any other.

- **Normalize black and brown childhood.** When you talk about children in general, pause that mental image. Are you picturing a black or brown child? Whiteness is default in our society, and that goes for how children are depicted on television, in books, in movies, and in our minds. The memes we share online, the cute cards with pictures of kids we give as gifts, our cherubs, our child stars, the precocious kids in our family comedies—they are all almost exclusively white. We celebrate the complex lives of white children, when they are good and bad, cute and exhausting. We see them as whole children. But children of color are rarely depicted that way, as complex individuals in their own environment. We don't see how black kids play together in our movies, we don't see how black parents raise their kids on our televisions. We are, as a species, biologically and culturally predisposed to nurture our children, but when our society only defines "children" as young people of a certain skin color, it can prevent some from seeing children of color as children to be loved and protected. I will never forget when twelve-year-old Tamir Rice was shot to death by a police officer in a park for holding a toy gun on November 22, 2014. Cleveland Police Union President Steve Loomis later remarked in response to the outcry and heartbreak over the death of a twelve-year-old boy, "He's menacing. He's 5-feet-7, 191 pounds. He wasn't that little kid you're seeing in pictures. He's a 12-year-old in an adult body." I can guarantee that to his mother, to his family, to his community—Tamir Rice was a child, a precious child, just like any twelve-year-old white boy is allowed to be.

- **Challenge language that stereotypes black and brown kids.** How often have you heard people talk of "thugs" or "hoodlums" or "gangbangers" and known almost immediately that they were talking about black and brown youth? Our children are criminalized in casual conversation every day. Their swagger is analyzed, the sag of their pants pathologized—we cannot let any of this slide. This is not just how random strangers see our children, it's how our teachers see our children, our police officers see our children, our juries see our children, and our politicians see our children. Challenge the stereotyping of black and brown youth, and the criminalization of black and brown youth culture. A swagger is not intent, baggy jeans are not intent, a bandana is not intent. This is culture, and any suggestion otherwise is racist.

- **Discuss deeper causes of defiant and antisocial behavior in black and brown youth.** If you find yourself in a discussion on the "problems of black and brown youth" don't let it stay on the surface. When white kids get in trouble, we don't launch into discussions of "what is wrong with white kids"—we ask things like, "What does this kid need? What is keeping this kid from thriving?" Resist attempts to treat the behavior of black and brown children as both the cause and symptom of the problems they may be facing in schools.
- **Don't erase disabled black and brown youth.** While black youth are more likely to be labeled as disabled when they are exhibiting social issues in school, once labeled, disabled black and brown youth are often left out of discussions on the school-to-prison pipeline altogether. Disabled kids of color are the most likely to be made victims of overly punitive school discipline and criminalization. Further, once criminalized, disabled people of color are more likely to face brutality by police. Our special education programs are failing the vast majority of disabled children—especially disabled children of color, and this must be addressed if we want to stop the criminalization of black and brown youth.
- **Challenge the legitimacy of white-centered education.** The truth is, so long as our children are being taught by white teachers, being taught by schools focused on the needs of white children, learning from textbooks teaching white culture, and taking tests designed for white students, our children of color are going to have a hard time engaging with and succeeding in schools. We must chal-

lenge the assumption that having our children succeed in a white supremacist school system is the best we can hope for, for kids of any race. We need to ask for truly diverse and inclusive education for all of our kids.

We often focus on the outcomes of the school-to-prison pipeline as the ultimate tragedy—the high drop-out rates, future poverty and joblessness, the likelihood of repeated incarceration—but when I look at our school-to-prison pipeline, the biggest tragedy to me is the loss of childhood joy. When our kids spend eight hours a day in a system that is looking for reasons to punish them, remove them, criminalize them—our kids do not get to be kids. Our kids do not get to be rambunctious, they do not get to be exuberant, they do not get to be rebellious, they do not get to be defiant. Our kids do not get to fuck up the way other kids get to; our kids will not get to look back fondly on their teenage hijinks—because these get them expelled or locked away. Do not wait until black and brown kids are grown into hurt and hardened adults to ask "What happened? What can we do?" We cannot give back childhoods lost. Help us save our children now.

nine

Why can't I say the "N" word?

THE FIRST TIME I WAS CALLED A NIGGER I WAS ELEVEN. My mother had a business trip for a week, and as a single mom, had to find a place to put my brother Aham and I. We were sent to her friend Liz's house in the town of Goldbar, about two hours' drive from our apartment. We were excited for the visit—Goldbar, a small town nestled in the mountains, was drastically different from our depressing apartment complex surrounded by strip malls. This was a rare chance for us to climb rocks and wade in a river. Liz and her husband's house was a large log cabin with floor-to-ceiling windows looking out on tall trees. Our windows just looked out on other apartments.

When we arrived at the house, Aham and I said goodbye to our mom, plopped our bags on the floor, and set out exploring with Liz's kids, Amy and Nick. Outside of the typical annoyances of being guests in someone's house, the first few days were glorious. We scaled giant rock faces (which I'm sure to my now adult eye would only look about 10 feet tall), we built stick forts, we played hide-and-seek and pretended that we were the last people on earth. At night, I'd climb into a sleeping bag on Amy's bedroom floor and we'd giggle about boys.

The weekend came to a close and Monday morning Liz suggested that we walk Nick and Amy to the school bus. Aham and I were both pretty excited about this. Maybe we'd make more friends and we'd all play together after school! We walked down the gravel road and waited together at the next street. When the bus pulled up we waved goodbye to Nick and Amy and eagerly looked in the bus windows at the other kids as Nick and Amy made their way to the bus. Some of the windows were down in the warm morning.

"Look!" one of the kids shouted. "Look, niggers!"

It took me a second to realize what had just been said. I'd only heard that word said in movies by hateful southerners and slave owners. But before it could fully register, another kid shouted.

"Ha! Look at the niggers!"

Within seconds, before Nick and Amy had even climbed on the bus, there was a loud group of kids laughing and shouting at us out the back windows.

"Niggers! Niggers!"

The words hit like buckets of cold water. I tried not to shake.

I looked at Nick and Amy. They would know what to do, these were their friends. But they weren't saying anything and they weren't looking at us—they were laughing.

My brother and I watched silently in horror as the bus drove off, the kids' laughter echoing back at us down the road. We turned around and walked slowly back to the house. I don't think we talked about what had just happened. We didn't have the words to describe our first encounter with such hate.

The next morning, as Nick and Amy put their backpacks on, Aham and I stayed put at the table.

"Aren't you going to walk them to the bus?" Liz asked, when it became apparent that we weren't moving.

My brother shook his head and quietly said, "No, we don't want to."

We hadn't discussed this, but Aham knew that I felt the same.

Liz looked at her kids briefly and then at us.

"Why?" she demanded.

Aham looked at her, and then at Nick and Amy. "Just don't," he said, and shrugged.

Liz was instantly angry. "Oh, you think you're too good for us?" she sneered.

My brother and I both shook our heads. There was nothing we could say. We couldn't say, in front of Nick and Amy, "The kids all called us niggers and your children laughed." So we just sat silently and I tried not to cry.

"Your mom sure has spoiled you," she muttered. "Ungrateful little . . . " she muttered. "Go to school, kids," she snapped and then left the room.

We didn't know what to do, all we knew was that we had obviously done something very wrong.

For the rest of the week, we were afraid to leave the house. This town was not safe. What if we ran into those kids? Those kids who hated us? Those kids who shouted the same words that the Klan members on TV had said as they lynched people who looked like us? We didn't want to be out in the woods, we didn't want to go out on the river. We wanted to go home, to our dingy apartment complex where nobody called us nigger, where nobody laughed at our blackness.

But we couldn't go home, and our fear of the strangers outside had forced us to stay inside with a woman who now vehemently disliked us. For the rest of the week she watched us like a hawk, yelling about every misplaced dish or any neglected please or thank you. The rest of the week the words "spoiled" and "lazy" were hurled at us as if they were our names. Sensing the change in environment, Nick and Amy started acting more cool toward us, treating us as annoyances, rather than friends. They didn't want to play games or talk about friends, they just wanted us to leave.

At the end of the week our mom came to get us. We silently packed our things into the car and waved goodbye at Liz and her family. On the way home, mom told us about her business trip. It had been a great trip, hard work, but exciting—and her job had never sent her away before. This was as close to a vacation as she was going to get. Aham and I listened to our mom talk about her trip and silently agreed to not tell her about how our week had gone. Our mom didn't get a lot of trips away, and she didn't have very many friends. We didn't want to cause any more trouble.

WORDS HAVE POWER. WORDS ARE MORE THAN THEIR dictionary definition. The history of a word matters as long as the effects of that history are still felt. Take, for example, the history of the word "nigger." First simply a take on the Latin noun *niger* (black), the word became a slur used to demean black slaves in the US. From the 1700s on, the word "nigger" was used almost exclusively to express hatred. Nigger was a word shouted at black men, women, and children by slave masters as they lashed their backs with whips. Nigger was a word hollered by white men in pickup trucks as they chased down black kids. Nigger was a word repeated by men in white hoods as they got ready to burn a cross on the lawn of a black family. Nigger was a word spat at hanged black bodies. Nigger is a very powerful word with a very painful history.

As long as we have had the spoken word, language has been one of the first tools deployed in efforts to oppress others. Words are how we process the world, how we form our societies, how we codify our morals. In order to make injustice and oppression palatable in a world with words that say that such things are unacceptable, we must come up with new words to distance ourselves from the realities of the harm we are perpetrating on others. This is how black people—human beings—become niggers. All oppression in race, class, gender, ability, religion—it all began with words.

Not all words are equally powerful, because not all words have the same history. Take the word "cracker." Cracker is a slur sometimes used to refer to white people. Many white people have argued that it is just as bad as using the word "nigger." But say both words aloud right now—loudly, which one turns your stomach? That feeling in your gut when you say the word "nigger" loudly and clearly, that is the history of the word being invoked with it as well. Cracker simply does not have that. Cracker does not invoke the mass lynchings of white people, "blacks only" lunch counters, snarling police dogs aimed at white bodies—because that simply did not happen in our history. Cracker has not been a tool of racial oppression against white people, because nobody is or has been racially oppressing white people (note: if this is where you say "what about the Irish" note that the word "cracker" certainly played absolutely no part in the oppression of the Irish, and that oppression was perpetrated by other white people).

In our history of racism, words have had a starring role in the brutalization of people of color. Beyond "nigger" and beyond black America, words have been used in the oppression of many races. I will not use those words here, because I am a black woman, and I do not feel comfortable invoking the painful history of words used to oppress Native American people, Asian American people, Latinx people, and more, when my community has not had to suffer the consequences of how those words have been used to justify genocide, internment camps, and more. But, looking at American history, words have been used to separate, dehumanize, and oppress, and the power of those words is still felt today. Picture a water fountain with the sign "colored" on it. Picture a lunch counter sign declaring, "Whites Only." Picture a group of angry white men encircling a terrified black boy, shouting, "white power." Think of the words used to subtly signify race. Words like ghetto, nappy, uppity, articulate, thug. All of these words can conjure up powerful emotions because they conjure up the powerful history, and present, that they have helped create.

People of color have inherited the pain of these words. The oppression they face today is a direct result of how these words were used in the past. Today, black people are still suffering from the ghettoization, poverty, police brutality, and everyday discrimination that these words helped build.

In contrast, white people have inherited the privilege that these words made possible. They have inherited the advantage of not having, in this generation and previous, the specific set of disadvantages placed in their way that these words placed on the lives of people of color. This is why, even if some of these words have been "reclaimed" by some in the community they were used to oppress, when these words are used by white people, that use will continue to be abusive. Because they are still benefitting from how these words have been used while people of color still suffer.

Does this mean that a well-meaning white person who is not trying to oppress people of color, absolutely cannot use these words—just because others may have had ill intent? No, you are free to say just about anything you want in a country with free speech. And even if people of color wanted to force someone to stop, we have very little power to do so. But the important question is, why would a well-meaning white person want to say these words in the first place? Why would you want to invoke that pain on people of color? Why would you want to rub in the fact that you are privileged enough to not be negatively impacted by the legacy of racial oppression that these words helped create?

A lot of people want to skip ahead to the finish line of racial harmony. Past all this unpleasantness to a place where all wounds are healed and the past is laid to rest. I believe that this is where some of the desire (excluding openly racist assholes who just want to make people of color feel unsafe) to use racially taboo language comes from. But words only lose their power when first the impact of those words are no longer felt, not the other way around. We live in a world where the impacts of systemic racism are still threatening the lives of countless people of color today.

Yes, this does mean that people of color can freely say some words that white people cannot without risking scorn or condemnation. That may seem very unfair to some, maybe even to you.

But it is fair.

It is completely fair that a word used to help create and maintain the oppression of others for your benefit would not be able to be used by you without invoking that oppression, while people of color who had never had the power to oppress with those words would be able to use them without invoking that same oppression.

The real unfairness lies in the oppression and inequality that these words helped create and maintain.

"Just get over it," some people say, as if the pain of racial oppression is a switch you can just turn off.

You can't "get over" something that is still happening. Which is why black Americans can't "get over" slavery or Jim Crow. It may be quite a while—likely past all of our lifetimes— before white people will be able to say "nigger" without harming black people.

So yes, the fact that people of color can say words that white people can't *is* an example of injustice—but it's not injustice against white people.

ten

What is cultural appropriation?

IF YOU TRAVEL A LOT, YOU BEGIN TO UNDERSTAND THE importance of airport food. When you are frazzled, frustrated from long lines, and nervous about your upcoming time in a metal capsule hurtling through the air, airport food can be the much-needed pause to collect yourself and feel human—or the final indignity that sends you to tears. And so it was, at the airport for my third trip of a very busy week, that I thought I'd found the respite that I desired.

I had spent the entire week driving from city to city eating fast food and disgusting edible cardboard from gas stations in my job as a marketing consultant. In the airports, I'd been lucky to find food that hadn't been shipped in prepackaged and then microwaved into a rubbery mass, and I'd have been even luckier if said restaurant sold a glass of wine fresh from a Franzia box. So by the time my last trip of the week had arrived, I was sick to death of travel food. But I'd been running around in meetings all morning and hadn't been able to eat properly before leaving for the airport. After having to return home ten minutes after leaving the house, realizing I'd left both my laptop charger and underwear at home, I'd fought torturous traffic, stood through the long security lines, took off my shoes, stood in the scanners, and finally made it to my gate with my bags, a tiny piece of my sanity, and a cavernous hunger.

Having safely located my gate and reassuring myself that I had enough time, I searched for a place to grab a quick bite and a glass of wine. I would catch my breath and the board the plane with a little less anxiety than had followed me through airport security. Provided I could find the right place to eat. This was not a gate I was used to, it was far off at the end of a terminal, where the nice seated restaurants are often replaced with vending machines. But I had hope. And after a few minutes, I found what I was looking for.

I found better than what I was looking for.

I found Africa Lounge.

Could this be? Had I possibly found African food in a sea of stale bagels? What type of food might it be—West African? Ethiopian? We had a large Ethiopian population in the area. What a great idea, to put an African restaurant in the international airport and to showcase to new arrivals some of the ethnic and cultural diversity of the area and to make people of different backgrounds feel more welcome. Also, have you had African food? No matter which region you are sampling—it's delicious. I almost jogged over, smiling in excitement.

But as I got closer, the warning signs started to appear. Were those zebra print chairs? Oh no, was that a caveman mural on the wall? My joy was rapidly plummeting.

The menu was placed on a placard out front. I took a look with a small bit of remaining hope

Bacon & Swiss Burger. . . . hmm, okay not that.

Grilled Italian Chicken. . . . nope.

I scanned further and quickly saw that there would be no African food. No fried plantain, no kitfo, no egusi soup. This wasn't an African restaurant; it was an American restaurant with "African-themed decor." And a pretty sad one at that.

And suddenly, I was very sad. I thought of the amazing African food I'd grown up with, and the few African restaurants I'd been able to find in the Pacific Northwest. Food that most white people had probably never reveled in the way I had. Food that wouldn't be able to command the prices that four-star restaurants would, even though just as much time, care, and skill went into its preparation. Restaurants that would always be expected to be a "bargain" until they were helmed by white chefs who drastically Americanized their menus and called it "fusion" so they could impress food critics. I thought of the Ethiopian restaurant that my mom's best friend used to own. I remembered watching her spread large circles of batter on a griddle to make fermented bread (injera) to eat with spiced lentils cooked in butter. I told all of my friends about how great Ethiopian food was even though I knew that there was a good chance I'd be met with the tired joke, "They have food in Ethiopia?" I thought of the really amazing Nigerian restaurant I used to go to years ago. It had to shut down because there weren't enough West Africans in the area to bring in the revenue it needed. I had loved taking my oldest son there, to a restaurant filled with traditional West African décor. Showing my son how to roll his fufu into round balls to dip in his stew. The room smelled like my childhood, and the music brought me back to memories of slightly tipsy Nigerian men dancing in my childhood living room, full of Jollof rice and happiness. But Nigerian food hadn't been popularized here yet—that is just beginning in the US within the last couple of years. I thought about how great it would be to come across a restaurant like that in an international airport. What a great way to show how international an American city could be.

But instead what I was standing in front of in that airport was a caricature of my culture. A caricature of the vibrant decorations and festive music. Everything I'd loved about African food had been skinned and draped around the shoulders of a glorified McDonalds. This was as close to African food as I was going to get here, and it was going to be served to me by a white man, in front of a caveman mural, and it would come with nachos.

ONE OF THE TRICKIEST CONVERSATIONS YOU'RE BOUND to have regarding race in America will likely be about cultural appropriation. While not as charged as "racist" or "privileged," "cultural appropriation" is a term that carries a lot of emotion and confusion for many people of all races.

At its core, cultural appropriation is about ownership of one's culture, and since culture is defined *both* collectively and individually, the definition and sentiment about cultural appropriation changes with one's identification and sentiment about aspects of their culture.

If that last sentence sounded really complicated, that's because it is—and it becomes easy to see why cultural appropriation has been a difficult concept for many. But let's attempt to simplify what we can, so that even if we can't agree on everything about cultural appropriation, we can perhaps agree on some ways to discuss it.

We can broadly define the concept of cultural appropriation as the adoption or exploitation of another culture by a more dominant culture. This is not usually the wholesale adoption of an entire culture, but usually just attractive bits and pieces that are taken and used by the dominant culture. Some modern and fairly well known examples of cultural appropriation by the dominant white culture in the West are things like the use of American Indian headdresses as casual fashion, the use of the bindi as an accessory, the adoption of belly-dancing into fitness routines, and basically every single "ethnic" Halloween costume.

In recent years, people of color have been able to draw more attention to the issue of cultural appropriation and the harm it causes, but it is still a concept that rubs many white people (and a few people of color) the wrong way. Many of us who were raised in the US were raised to think of America as a "melting pot." Our beauty and our strength came from the exchange of cultures in this nation of immigrants. Aren't we supposed to be appreciating other cultures? Doesn't this *fight* racism?

These sentiments are certainly understandable, but they err in conflating appreciation with appropriation. Appreciation should benefit all cultures involved, and true appreciation does. But appropriation, more often than not, disproportionately benefits the dominant culture that is borrowing from marginalized cultures, and can even harm marginalized cultures.

What is cultural appropriation?

The problem of cultural appropriation is not in the desire to participate in aspects of a different culture that you admire. The problem of cultural appropriation is primarily linked to the power imbalance between the culture doing the appropriating and the culture being appropriated. That power imbalance allows the culture being appropriated to be distorted and redefined by the dominant culture and siphons any material or financial benefit of that piece of culture away to the dominant culture, while marginalized cultures are still persecuted for living in that culture. Without that cultural power imbalance, cultural appropriation becomes much less harmful.

Even if a culturally appropriative act means to respect culture, it cannot if it can't understand and respect the past and present power dynamics defining that culture's interaction with the dominant culture.

Let's look at the ever-tired example of rap music. Rap music was born from the rhythmic storytelling tradition of West Africa. Brought to the West by slaves, these rhythmic words wove their way through blues, jazz, and call-and-response and eventually birthed rap. From West Africa through slavery, the horror of the post-Reconstruction era, Jim Crow segregation, post-Reagan mass-incarceration—music has provided solace, hope, release, and strength to black people. And for all that black music gave to black Americans, it was not respected by white America. Blues, jazz, and rock were all deemed dangerous and unseemly forms of music at one time. Even as the art forms grew in popularity, the black musicians who performed them were treated like servants, often forced to enter and exit white-only clubs through the service entrance, to perform for crowds of white-only faces, for fees at a fraction of what white performers could command. The gain in popularity did little to increase the respectability of black music, until white artists began imitating it—and then most of the respectability and fame was given to the white artists. Think of artists like Elvis Presley who have been canonized in the annals of music history for work that was lifted almost wholesale from the backs of black musicians whose names most Americans will never know.

Rap has been long vilified by many in "respectable" white America. It is the language of "thugs" and is responsible for numerous societal ills from "black-on-black" crime to single-parenthood. Rap music is the reason why your teenager is suddenly disrespectful. Rap music is the reason why kids don't go to church anymore. Wife leave you? Pretty sure rap music told her to.

Rap is, in reality, a difficult and beautiful art form that requires not only musical and rhyming talent, but a mathematically complex sense of timing. Rap is a very diverse art form that can entertain, inform, enrage, comfort, and inspire. Like many art forms, many people will spend their entire lives working at it and will never be better than mediocre. Some, with rare talent, will rise to the top, others with rare talent will continue to toil in obscurity. But if you are a white rapper, you can be "okay" and go multi-platinum. Not only can a halfway decent white rapper sell millions of copies of a halfway decent album, raking in money that most black artists would never dream of, that white rapper is more likely to be accepted as "mainstream."

That "legitimacy" bestowed by whiteness actually changes the definition of rap for the American culture. When the most popular rappers in the country are white rappers doing a decent impersonation of black master rappers, what kids see as legitimate rap changes. What they aspire to changes. Whom they give their money to changes. When these same white rappers are given Grammys for their attempts, over more talented black rappers, it makes it harder for rap by black artists to be accepted by mainstream culture—because it sounds different than what they've come to know as "good rap."

And in all of this, the music that we see on television and hear on our radio is further divorced from the struggle and triumph that inspired it from Africa, through slavery, and through today. The art form that black Americans have relied upon for generations is no longer theirs. While the struggle remains.

So does this mean that if you are white, you should never rap? Should that avenue just never be open to you? This is the type of question that fuels the most heated debate around cultural appropriation.

First off, let's acknowledge that you can do whatever you want. You can rap, you can belly dance, you can do anything allowed by law. But whether you "can" or "should" do something is a different matter—that it may be racially insensitive or harmful is beside the point. You can. If you are reading this book, I'm assuming you are doing so because you *don't want to harm or offend people of other races.* And there's a good chance that at least part of you is hoping that not harming others will also not cause you to have to give up too much of the social and cultural activities you have long enjoyed. But I'm not here to absolve you or condemn you for your rap aspirations.

And even if the question of whether or not you could become the world's greatest white rapper hadn't just been answered, it would be completely beside the point. Continuing to look at rap as an example of cultural appropriation verses cultural appreciation: if you really love rap, you love more than just the beats. You love the artists, the pioneers, the science, the history of it all. You love the meaning and the significance of rap—not only what it has meant to you, but what it has meant to the artists and its fans. If you love rap you love the strength it has provided black people. If you love rap you understand that it is an art form that has been lovingly grown and nurtured in a hostile world. You also understand that the pain and adversity that helped shape rap is not something you've had to face. When you look at the history of rap, the heritage of rap, the struggle of rap, the triumph of rap—it may inspire you to want to rap yourself. But when all you can take is the art, and you can take the enjoyment and the profit and the recognition—and you can't take any of the pain or the history or the struggle, can you do so and honestly call it rap if you love it at all?

But there's an even bigger point to be recognized in all of this. Cultural appropriation is the product of a society that prefers its culture cloaked in whiteness. Cultural appropriation is the product of a society that only respects culture cloaked in whiteness. Without that—if all culture (even the culture that appropriators claim to love and appreciate) were equally desired and respected, then imitations of other cultures would look like just that—imitations. If all cultures were equally respected, then wearing a feathered headdress to Coachella would just seem like the distasteful decision to get trashed in sacred artifacts. If all cultures were equally respected, then white college kids with dreadlocks would look like middle-class white kids wearing the protest of poor blacks against the suppression, degradation, and oppression of white colonialists as costumes. But we don't live in a society that equally respects all cultures, which is why what would otherwise be seen as offensive and insensitive behavior, is instead treated as a birthright of white Americans. And because we do not live in a society that equally respects all cultures, the people of marginalized cultures are still routinely discriminated against for the same cultural practices that white cultures are rewarded for adopting and adapting for the benefit of white people. Until we do live in a society that equally respects all cultures, any attempts of the dominant culture to "borrow" from marginalized cultures will run the risk of being exploitative and insulting.

That doesn't seem fair on the surface, that we'd have to wait for a better world before we can start borrowing and adapting from other cultures with abandon. And it does not seem fair to those who feel that other cultures can take from white culture without the same risk of being labeled appropriative. But what actually is not fair, is the expectation that a dominant culture can just take and enjoy and profit from the beauty and art and creation of an oppressed culture, without taking on any of the pain and oppression people of that culture had to survive while creating it.

But who defines what is sacred to a culture? Who defines what was born of struggle? Who defines what is off limits? This is where things get complicated. What is offensive to one person in a marginalized culture, is not offensive to another. Some practices have been shared with white culture so long, and the emotional connection to the founding culture is so far changed, that for most, the question of appropriation is moot. And this is where the anxiety lies, because when you are trying to not appropriate a culture, but also trying to live in a diverse world, it can be hard to know what is or is not going to offend. And it can also be hard to be a part of the oppressed culture, and stand up for your ownership over your cultural art and practices, and know that other people from your culture may disagree with you and give permission for what is sacred to you to be used and changed.

However this debate plays out for the individual situations you may find yourself in, know that it cannot end well if it does not start with enough respect for the marginalized culture in question to listen when somebody says "this hurts me." And if that means that your conscience won't allow you to dress as a geisha for Halloween, know that even then, in the grand scheme of things—you are not the victim.

eleven

Why can't I touch your hair?

I LOVE MY HAIR. IT'S FLUFFY AND CURLY AND BIG. I'VE spent years nurturing it to glory; so much care and so many products and hours of YouTube tutorials have left me with hair that I love more than I love candy or cheesecake. I love taking selfies of my hair and talking about my hair, and if you ask, I will probably let you touch it because it's very, very soft. But I wasn't prepared to be talking about my hair on the first day of my new job.

I had worked my ass off for a promotion. It was a coveted new position with the company I worked for. I'd beaten out hundreds of my coworkers (and even a few of the managers) for this role, and after weeks of interviews and sleepless nights, I'd accepted the role and was finally meeting my new team. The rest of the team flew in from around the country for our initial training. We met for dinner and drinks that first evening at a local restaurant.

In a team of over twenty, I was the only black person at the table. But it didn't really bother me. I was used to that working in the tech industry in Seattle. That's the way it was.

We talked about our respective hometowns, about our families, and about our excitement over our new jobs. I was smiling and laughing with my teammates when the director of our division—my boss's boss—spoke loudly from across the long table.

"Is that your real hair?" he asked.

I heard his voice but his words didn't really register as I was in the middle of conversation with a coworker about his hometown in the South. But people had stopped talking and I realized that the director had been talking to me.

I turned my head toward him. "Hmm?" I asked.

"I said, is that your real hair?" he repeated.

If it was possible for a silent table to get even more silent, that is what happened. Everyone stared at me with curiosity while I tried to figure out the best way to answer this question. I decided to go with simplicity.

"Yes, it is," I answered. Hoping that would be the end of it.

"I'm glad it's not one of those weaves," he continued on, giving approval to my personal beauty choice, "Those are so expensive and really bad for your hair."

Oh my god, why? Why was this happening to me? What prank television show was I on?

I smiled weakly, "Yeah, hair can be a big deal to some people." Hoping it would suffice.

Then came the question I was dreading.

"Have you seen that Chris Rock movie about hair?"

No, I haven't seen that Chris Rock movie about hair. I don't need to see a Chris Rock movie about black hair when I have my own head of black hair for reference. But if I had $1 for every white person who has asked me if I've seen that movie and then proceeded to educate me on the problems with my own damn hair and the black hair industry I'd have enough money to keep myself in Indian Remy for life.

A coworker joined in, "I saw that movie, too. Those chemicals people put in their hair are very dangerous!" She looked at me with both concern and fascination.

I just sat there in silence, reminding myself that I needed this damn job so I needed to just smile at this man and maybe have another drink.

"Spending hundreds of dollars a month on your hair. You got bills to pay! It's ridiculous!" he continued, oblivious to my great discomfort. I couldn't say any more. I felt like if I were to open my mouth, I might wail. So I just pleasantly stared until my next drink arrived and my director got bored and moved conversation back to the teammate sitting next to him.

Every month of my childhood, my mom would slather my hair and scalp with burning chemicals. As the chemical solution worked to break the bonds of the curls in my hair, along with removing the top layers of skin on my scalp, I would try not to cry. "It hurts!" I would complain to my mother, to which my mother would reply, "Do you want it straight or not?"

And I did want my hair straight. While my mom preferred my hair in its naturally curly kinky state, I wanted long, straight hair. I wanted the hair I saw on shampoo commercials, the hair I saw in magazines, the hair that boys would want to run their fingers through. I didn't want my stiff, coarse hair that didn't move in the breeze. I didn't want my hair that kids called nappy and ugly. I wanted to be a beautiful girl, and beautiful girls did not have hair like mine. So every month I tried to burn the blackness out of my hair, and I would then run a hot comb over it, ignoring the stench of burning protein while trying to avoid further injury to my bleeding and scabbed scalp.

And still my hair didn't sway in the breeze, and it never grew below my shoulders without breaking off in burned clumps.

But I didn't have money for the best solution, the solution of just covering up my hair that refused to be beautiful with long flowing hair of unknown origin. So I had to settle for stiff hair burned, sprayed, and pinned into poor replicas of the styles I saw in magazines. By the time I reached the age of thirty, I had no memory of what my natural hair looked like, all I knew was the disappointment I felt when I looked in the mirror.

When natural hair started to become popular again, I took a leap and cut my chemically processed hair off. I was not comfortable with very short hair, and spent that entire year feeling self-conscious. But I love a project, and I made loving my hair a personal goal. I set to it and succeeded. And as my hair grew out into fluffy coils I was finally proud of what I saw when I looked in the mirror. My hair still wasn't what I saw in commercials or in magazines, but it was mine—no longer dictated by the preferences of White America—and it was beautiful.

And after decades of pain associated with my hair, after decades of self-consciously patting it down after it became too "poufy" in the rain, after decades of damage and manipulation, after finally breaking free from the expectations, after resisting the pressure to conform, my hair was still a source of shame. Here was my director singling me out, in front of my coworkers, not to shame me, but to shame other black women for making different choices than I was now making. To shame other black women for spending a lot of money to not have to have the embarrassing and demeaning conversation I was now being forced to have. He wanted me to know that he approved of my hair, hair that, finally, was existing outside of his beauty norms. But still, he thought that my hair, growing on my head, from my body, was within his jurisdiction. Still, my hair would be a tool of oppression, even if it was to belittle other black women. My hair still existed for his use. Even then, even in a state as removed from whiteness as it could be, my hair was not my own.

IF YOU ARE WHITE, THERE'S A GOOD CHANCE THAT I know almost as much about your hair as you do. I know how to wash and condition it, I know all the different styles you can use. I know about mousse and hairspray and fishtail braids and that sea salt spray you can use to create that "tousled" look. I know about all the brushes and combs and the teasing and blowouts. Because your hair is everywhere. In every movie and television show. There are detailed how-to's in every fashion magazine. The hair of a famous white woman can become a style sensation. I remember "The Rachel." Because your hair is "good" hair. Your hair is the hair represented in the haircare aisles at stores. Your hair is the shining example of health in the shampoo commercials.

But it is very likely, if you are not black, that you know very little about my hair. You do not know about my pomades and co-wash, my Denmans and hot combs, my bantu knots and braid-outs. You don't know why I need so many bobby pins, why I put oil over my hair, why wash day is indeed an entire day. Because my hair is not the stuff of commercials or of fashion fantasy. My hair is a mystery on my head, just beyond your reach.

I catch people staring longingly at my curls, wanting desperately to make that reach. If I know and like the person, and if I'm in a good mood and my style can withstand it, I'll sometimes offer up a feel to a curious friend. "It's okay, you can touch it," I say, quickly adding, "But don't get any ideas." But often, I don't let people touch my hair. Those who do without asking will receive a range of responses, depending on how safe I feel to speak out. But you will never ever get a smile from me for it. I've had clerks touch my hair at stores, servers touch my hair at restaurants, bosses touch my hair at company parties. And it is never okay, because they never got permission.

I'm not the only black person who has a special dislike for uninvited hair touching. When I asked my friends of color what some of their least favorite microaggressions were, hair touching came up time and time again with my black friends. We do not like it. And it's happening far too often.

Hair is, biologically, dead the moment it begins to grow out of your head. It has no feelings, no sentience. To cut off our hair would not cause us any physical pain. So why is hair-touching such a big deal? Here are some reasons.

- **Touching anybody anywhere without their permission or a damn good reason is just not okay.** We teach our kids about personal space for a reason. If you wouldn't walk up and touch a random person on the back why would you touch their hair? Don't touch people who do not want to be touched.
- **It's weird.** Hair is growing out of somebody's body, coated in different beauty products and a fair amount of sweat and oil. Touching someone else's hair is weird and gross. Everybody seems to get that when someone else's hair is found anywhere—on a seat, on a hotel pillow, in your food—anywhere except on the head of a black person.
- **Hands are dirty.** You didn't wash them. Get them and all their germs away from the hair that is literally inches from my face.
- **Curls are precious.** That hairstyle that you are trying to send your hands into took more time than your life is worth (okay, not really . . . but try me and see). Stranger hands bring frizz and destroy curl patterns, and I will not have it.
- **It is a continuation of the lack of respect for the basic humanity and bodily autonomy of black Americans that is endemic throughout White Supremacy.** Allow me to elaborate.

Since the first black Americans were brought over as slaves, our bodies have not been our own. We were objects—property. Our bodies were curiosities and tools to be inspected and exploited. Our bodies were sources of judgment and shame. But they were never beautiful, and they were never our own.

Whatever respect we could get in White America came from how closely we could get our bodies to resemble those of white people. If our mothers were raped by white men and we were born with lighter skin, we could almost be seen as attractive. If our hair was pressed stiff and straight with burning irons, or irreparably broken with toxic chemicals, we might be seen as a credit to our race—we were, after all, trying to be less black. And we tried to express ourselves within these rules, tried to enjoy our bodies and our hair within these rules. But mostly, we have just wanted to go about our day without the reminder that our bodies and our hair are found "brutish" and "ugly" or "fascinating" and "exotic." We still live in a country where our hair is seen as "wild," as "unattractive," as "unprofessional" as "ghetto." We still live in a country where our hair can cost us jobs, even our place in the military. We still live in a country where our hair determines how professional we seem, how respectable we seem—even how intelligent we seem. Our hair is used to help determine our place in a white supremacist society.

If you are not black, and you are tired of hair like mine being a mystery to you, there are a lot of ways to get to know more about our hair. You could ask why more black people with black hair aren't in more television shows and movies. You could ask why there are no "how-to's" for our hair in your magazines. You could ask why our hair products have to take up one tiny section of a completely different aisle in the store. You could ask why our hair isn't called beautiful, why our hairstyles aren't the ones you are coveting. But instead, you assume you could just touch it. Because it is not about equality or even understanding—it's about reaffirming that nothing and nobody is beyond your grasp.

Or maybe it's not that serious. Maybe you just want to know if my hair is as soft and fluffy as you imagined it to be. Trust me, it's even softer. But you still don't get to touch it—not without my permission. Because we still live in a world where little respect and autonomy is granted to black people, where we are constantly reminded of how little control over our lives we have. So maybe for now you set your curiosity aside and allow someone the space to determine who does or does not touch their hair, without labeling them rude, sensitive, or divisive.

If you have a loving, trusting relationship with a black person and you are sure they won't mind if you asked to touch their hair, you can consider it. But *really* consider what you are asking. Even though it is just hair—dead piles of keratin—as long as our hair and our bodies are judged and controlled and violated by White Supremacy, it will always be so much more.

twelve

What are microaggressions?

"WELL, YOU SHOULDN'T WEAR RED LIPSTICK ANY-
way. On your lips, you'd look like a clown."

Jennifer said this to me at the end of the lunch period in
our middle school. She was leaning against the wall, like a
cool girl from television. Jennifer had a horizontally striped
shirt that was all the rage in the early '90s and slightly slouchy
jeans that would only in later years be called "mom jeans"
but at the time were very "in." She had skin that I'd seen in
romantic novels referred to as "peaches and cream." Her au-
burn hair was in a stylish bob. And on her lips was a beautiful
shade of red lipstick.

My mom had just allowed me to begin wearing lipstick the
beginning of that seventh-grade year. But with all of my mom's
lectures on the importance of "natural" looking makeup, I
knew without asking that I would not be able to leave my
house with a bright red shade on my lips. In all honesty, I'd

never really thought about wearing red lipstick before, but seeing my too-cool classmate donning the shade informed me that I had been missing out on all that makeup had to offer.

I had walked over to Jennifer, pulled by her beauty. I tugged my yellow jacket that I used to hide my belly a little tighter over my body. My too-tight jeans made zipping noises and my chubby thighs rubbed together. I patted down the top of my relaxed hair with an inch of puffy roots. Jennifer was everything I was not, but I loved her lipstick, so we finally had something in common.

"I really like that lipstick," I said, trying to sound like I wasn't nervous, like Jennifer and I talked every day, "I wish my mom would let me wear a color like that."

Jennifer looked at me, smiled briefly, and then said, "Well, you shouldn't wear red lipstick anyway. On your lips, you'd look like a clown."

I broke into a cold sweat immediately. "Oh, yeah, heheh," I tried to laugh, "I guess you're right. My big lips."

I pinched my lips together, trying to draw them into my mouth. "Ok, see ya," I said with faked nonchalance and turned and walked away, patting my hair and tightening my jacket once again.

I didn't wear red lipstick until after I graduated high school. And not because of my mom.

I patted my hair all of the time because of all of the times my hair had been referred to as "poufy." Nothing bad was meant by it, nobody was trying to hurt. It was just an acknowledgement that in a time where people were literally coating their strands in silicone, my hair's volume was a noticeable and unpleasant contrast.

My hair and my lips were not the only part of me that was too much. I had taken on quite a babyish voice a few years earlier, after all of the jokes about how my loudness was so "typical for a black girl"—I didn't know what that meant, because I was the only black girl at my school, but I knew it wasn't good. My butt was also too big, that was made very clear with references to hip-hop songs glorifying large butts that were often recited to me by smiling classmates.

I would be having a good day, lost in my imagination, and bam—I'd be hit with a comment that would remind me that I was not allowed to get comfortable. I couldn't walk comfortably, I couldn't talk comfortably, I couldn't sit without patting my hair, I couldn't smile without worrying about how large my lips looked.

In spite of all of this, I did really love school. I was a bright kid who enjoyed learning. I was in the advanced program in middle school and finished the last two years of high school at the local community college to get a head start on college credit. I had been obsessed with getting into a good college. By ninth grade, I had an entire row on my bookshelf dedicated to college brochures. I wasn't the only one, other kids in the advanced classes were just as obsessed with college as I was.

At first, my eyes would light up when kids would start talking about college. Finally, something we all had in common. After hanging around the periphery of such talk for a few weeks, I finally decided to join in. I began rattling off the colleges that I had hoped to go to when a student cut me off and said, "I mean, you don't have to try that hard anyway do you? You're black, you don't even have to do well in school to get into college. You don't even have to be in this class."

He looked at me matter-of-factly when he said this, no malice in his eyes. The other kids in the group just sort of nodded to themselves as if this kid had said something as plainly true as "the earth is round." And although it hadn't been explicitly said, the message was clear, "You don't belong here." Even in this group of nerds, this group of people who loved the same boring books and random facts and all raced to be the first to answer the same questions in school as me, I didn't belong. Because I was black.

I would like to say that this is when I stopped caring what other people think, that this was when I stopped trying to fit in. But I was a fifteen-year-old girl, and I was so lonely. So I kept trying. I kept trying to make friends and build community and every time I thought I'd made progress, someone would deflate all of the air out of my dream.

But as painful as it was, I didn't know that it was wrong. I didn't know that I wasn't supposed to be treated this way. I was pretty sure that I was the problem. Because nobody came to my defense, hell, nobody batted an eye when these things were said to me. They weren't a big deal, just small comments, little jokes. I shouldn't be so sensitive. It was all in my head. If I just found a way to have less things wrong with me, these bothersome comments would stop. So I smiled less, ate less, laughed less, and spoke in a whisper.

My senior year I had been invited to a scholarship conference at a local university for promising students of color. I was very nervous. By then, almost all group social interaction sent me into a spiral of anxiety and depression—and I didn't know any of these kids at the conference. What if I fit in even less than I did at school? I almost didn't go, but the lure of a possible scholarship helped strengthen my resolve.

I arrived at the hotel conference room. Inside there were hundreds of black and brown students. More kids of color than I'd ever previously seen combined. I was immediately overwhelmed by the noise. Kids were laughing in loud, open-mouthed guffaws. Everybody was using their outdoor voice. People were slapping each other on the arm as they talked. Everybody looked like old friends. I looked at the long tables that students were seated at, like a school cafeteria. My stomach clenched. I hated school cafeterias. Nothing lets you know that you are going to die alone like when you try to find a seat in a school cafeteria and everyone avoids eye contact like you are walking flatulence. I edged closer to the tables and scanned the room, trying to look for open seats without making eye contact, so that nobody would have the chance to reject me by looking away.

After a few moments I heard a voice next to me, but it didn't really register. Then I heard it again.

"Hey! Come on. Are you going to sit or what?"

She was talking to me. I sat down gratefully next to her. She introduced herself and asked my name. "Ijeoma," I answered quietly.

"What?" she yelled over the din of the room.

I was going to have to use my real voice in here. "Ijeoma," I answered again, loudly.

One of the college program administrators began his welcoming speech. After a few minutes of rules and expectations, along with a congratulation for our current and future academic success, the administrator finally said the words that three hundred black and brown kids had been waiting for him to say.

"We have pizza for everyone."

There was an immediate dash to the table piled high with pizza boxes behind the administrators. Kids advanced upon that pizza like there was a winning lottery ticket at the bottom of every slice. But I didn't. Because I was a fat kid. I wasn't just a fat kid; I was a fat black kid. And I knew that rushing to eat the pizza that I so desperately wanted would confirm what was insinuated the many times I'd heard people say, "well at least you're black, they think fat women are attractive." What hadn't been said, but had been meant was, "It's not okay to be fat, but it's the most we can expect from a black girl."

I was so hungry. I hadn't eaten all day. I was just as hungry as every other kid cramming entire slices of pepperoni pizza into their mouths. The pizza smelled so good. I looked at all my options and worked out a plan. Vegetarian pizza. I would grab a single slice of vegetarian pizza. Then, even though I'd still be a fat black girl with pizza, I'd look like I was at least trying not to be. I walked over to the vegetarian pizza, there was no rush to these boxes. I opened a box and looked for a reasonable slice—one big enough so that I wouldn't pass out from low blood sugar within the hour, and one small enough to let people know that I already understood I wasn't supposed to be enjoying it.

As I reached for a piece, the girl who had invited me to sit next to her reached for a slice next to it. Then she drew her hand back as if it had bit her.

"Salad pizza?" she looked up at a nearby friend and shouted, "Girl look. They got salad pizza over here. Ha! I'm not eating salad pizza."

She walked off toward the pepperoni. Another kid shook his head and chuckled, "Salad pizza," to himself.

I closed the lid on the box, walked over to the pepperoni pizza, and grabbed two giant slices. And I ate, in public, without fear, for the first time in years.

Not once in the two days I was at the conference did anybody make fun of my name. Not once in the two-day conference did anybody even glance at my hair. Not once in the two-day conference was I aware of the loudness of my voice or the size of my ass. Not once in the two-day conference did anybody question the academic achievements that had brought me there—we were all there because we were smart kids who had worked very hard. For two days I got to feel like the majority of my classmates had felt almost every day, like a complete human being.

I don't know how to describe what those two days were like for me except to say that I hadn't known before then that there was so much air to breathe.

YOU KNOW THE HYPERCRITICAL PARENT IN THE MOVIES? The mom or dad who finds a way to cut you to the quick right when you are feeling happy or proud or comfortable? "Nice to see you're finally trying," or "That's a lovely dress. I can't even see how much weight you gained." The remark that seems harmless on the surface? The small sting that comes out of nowhere and is repeated over and over, for your entire life? That is what racial microaggressions are like, except instead of a passive-aggressive parent, it's the entire world, in all aspects of your life, and very rarely is it said with any misguided love.

Microaggressions are small daily insults and indignities perpetrated against marginalized or oppressed people because of their affiliation with that marginalized or oppressed group, and here we are going to talk about racial microaggressions—insults and indignities perpetrated against people of color. But microagressions are more than just annoyances. The cumulative effect of these constant reminders that you are "less than" does real psychological damage. Regular exposure to microaggressions causes a person of color to feel isolated and invalidated. The inability to predict where and when a microaggression may occur leads to hypervigilance, which can then lead to anxiety disorders and depression. Studies have shown that people subjected to higher levels of microaggressions are more likely to exhibit the mental and physical symptoms of depression.[1]

As harmful as microaggressions can be, they are very hard to address in real life. Why? Because they are very hard to see.

Microaggressions are small (hence, the "micro") and can be easily explained away. It is very easy to dismiss a small offense as a misunderstanding or simple mistake.

Microaggressions are cumulative. On their own, each microaggression doesn't seem like a big deal. But just like one random bee sting might not be a big deal, a few random bee stings every day of your life will have a definite impact on the quality of your life, and your overall relationship with bees.

Microaggressions are perpetrated by many different people. Because each microaggression is just one sting perpetrated by a different person, it is hard to address with each individual person without (1) becoming very exhausted, and (2) being written off as hypersensitive.

Many people do not consciously know that they are perpetrating a microaggression against someone. Much of our oppressive actions are done in complete ignorance of their effect, or subconsciously—where we aren't fully aware of why we are acting aggressively toward someone. This is often the case with microaggressions. Rarely does somebody perpetrating one say to themselves, "I'm going to find a small way to hurt this person."

Having established that microaggressions are hard to see, let's take a look at some of the ways in which they can show up in everyday conversations for people of color.

"Are you the first person in your family to graduate from college?"

"Are you an affirmative action hire?"

"Wow, you speak English really well."

"You aren't like other black people."

"I thought Asian people eat a lot of rice."

"Why do black people give their kids such funny names?"

"That's so ghetto."

"Is that your real hair? Can I touch it?"

"You listen to opera? I thought you were black."

"Wow, you're so articulate."

"Your name is too difficult for me. Do you have a nickname?"

What are microaggressions?

"Where are you from? No . . . I mean, where are your parents from? I mean . . . where is your name from?"

"Is the baby-daddy in the picture?"

"You have really big eyes for an Asian person."

"Why are you complaining? I thought Chinese people loved homework."

"Welcome to America."

"Do your kids all have the same dad?"

"You don't sound black."

"Are you the maid?"

"Excuse me, this is the first-class area."

"Is this a green card marriage?"

"You're so exotic."

"You have such a chip on your shoulder."

"Are you the nanny?"

"That fiery Latin blood."

"Did you grow up in a teepee?"

"Are you visiting this neighborhood?"

"Your accent is adorable."

Microaggressions aren't always delivered in words. It's the woman who grabs her purse as you walk by. The store clerk following you around to see if you need "help." The person speaking loudly and slowly to you because you probably don't understand English. The person locking their car doors as you walk past their vehicle. The high-end sales clerks who assume that you didn't come to shop. The fellow customers who assume you are an employee. The people who decide to "take the next elevator instead." The professor who asks to check your sources, and only *your* sources, "just to be sure." The kids whose parents say that they can't come play with your kid. The not-so-random random security checks at airports. The crowded bus where nobody will sit next to you. The cab that won't stop for you.

For nonwhites, racial microaggressions find a way into every part of every day.

Microaggressions are constant reminders that you don't belong, that you are less than, that you are not worthy of the same respect that white people are afforded. They keep you off balance, keep you distracted, and keep you defensive. They keep you from enjoying an outing on the town or a day at the office.

Microaggressions are a serious problem beyond the emotional and physical effects they have on the person they are perpetrated against. They have much broader social implications. They normalize racism. They make racist assumptions a part of everyday life. The assumption that a black father isn't in the picture reinforces an image of irresponsible black men that keeps them from being hired for jobs. The assumption that a Latinx woman doesn't speak good English keeps her from a promotion. The assumption that a child of color's parents wouldn't have a college degree encourages guidance counselors to set lower goals for that child. The assumption that black people are "angry" prevents black people from being taken seriously when airing legitimate grievances. These microaggressions help hold the system of White Supremacy together, because if we didn't have all these little ways to separate and dehumanize people, we'd empathize with them more fully, and then we'd have to really care about the system that is crushing them.

What are microaggressions?

WHEN SOMEBODY HAS PERPETRATED A MICROAGGRESSION against you, it can be hard to address. There is no guaranteed method for success that will make somebody realize what they are doing and stop, but here are a few strategies that work at least part of the time.

- **State what actually happened.** Some things just need to be called what they are, and microaggressions are definitely among those things. "You just assumed that I don't speak English." Say it directly. What is happening to you is real and you have every right to name it.
- **Ask some uncomfortable questions.** Because a lot of microaggressions are perpetrated with subconscious motivation, questioning the action can force someone to really examine their motives. Two of my favorites are "Why did you say that?" and "I don't get it. Please clarify."
- **Ask some more uncomfortable questions.** If the person you are talking to becomes flustered or insists they meant nothing by it, ask, "Is this something you would have said to a white person?" or "How exactly was I supposed to take what you just said?"
- **Reinforce that good intentions are not the point.** "You may not have meant to offend me, but you did. And this happens to people of color all the time. If you do not mean to offend, you will stop doing this."
- **Remember, you are not crazy and you have every right to bring this up.** "I can see this is making you uncomfortable, but this is a real problem that needs to be addressed."

If you witness racial microaggressions against someone else, you should strongly consider speaking out as well—especially if you are a white person. The strategies above will also work when confronting microaggressions against other people, with a few minor tweaks to ensure that you aren't making this about—well, you. Also, please take the lead of the person of color who is being directly harmed by the microaggression. If it seems like they do not want the issue addressed, do not decide to come to their rescue anyway—people of color have very good reasons for why they choose to speak out and why they choose not to, and you don't want to remove that agency from them. It is also important to make sure that when confronting microaggressions against others, you are not doing so in a way that will place the person of color you are defending at greater risk or will increase the burden on them. Don't make enemies for them—help when you are reasonably confident that you can do some good. And if that person of color is already speaking out and looks like they could use some support, offer it! It's a horrible feeling to speak out against microaggressions in a room full of white people and be met with nothing but hostility or silence.

As a person of color, you don't have to call out every microaggression against you, but you have the right to call out each and every one that you choose to. Do not let people convince you that you are being oversensitive, that you are being disruptive or divisive. What is harmful and divisive are these acts of aggression against people of color that are allowed to happen constantly, without consequence. What is harmful and divisive is the expectation that people of color would just accept abuse. While sometimes these conversations about mi-

croaggressions can be very healthy and lead to a pleasant resolution, where a well-meaning person genuinely listens and
acknowledges the pain they've caused, often, the person you
are talking with will refuse to see what you are saying and will
become defensive. And that's okay. Even that is progress.

Because these harmful actions should not be comfortable.
And if you get called out enough times, you'll stop, if only to
be able to go about your day without argument. And eventually, for many people, it does sink in—maybe not the first
time, or the fifth time, but eventually. It is not your job as
a person of color to educate people on their racist actions,
please remember that, but it is always your right to stand up
for yourself when you choose to.

If you have been called out for a racist microaggression,
and you want to understand and you do not want to hurt
people of color, here are some tips:

- **Pause.** It is very easy to be overwhelmed with emotions
  when you are called out. Before you respond at all, pause
  and catch your breath and remember that your goal is
  to understand and to have a better relationship with the
  person you are talking to.
- **Ask yourself: "Do I really know why I said/did that?"**
  Think for a moment—why did you choose to make that
  comment? Why did you clutch at your purse? If you can't
  think of a good reason, this is a good sign that you should
  examine this more in yourself.
- **Ask yourself: "Would I have said this to somebody of
  my race? Is it something I say to people of my race?"** If
  it's a comment that is specific to that race (say, assuming

that a Chinese American doesn't like "American" food), ask yourself if you think of and voice similar stereotypes in your everyday interactions with other white people. When a white person orders Chinese, do you say, "But I thought you only ate hot dogs!"?

- **Ask yourself if you were feeling threatened or uncomfortable in the situation, and then ask yourself why.** Often, microaggressions are a defense mechanism when people are feeling racial tension. You're hanging out with your buddies and then a black friend comes and joins a previously all-white table. That discomfort might cause you to act inappropriately, acknowledging that the mood has been changed because someone "different" who doesn't quite belong has joined. But instead of investigating your own biases and prejudice that make you uncomfortable, you take it out on the person who joined by making the difference their problem with a racially insensitive joke or reference. Sometimes, you feel challenged by a person of color and your defense is to "knock them down a peg or two" and you do that by referencing their race in a negative or isolating manner—you don't know that's why when you do it, but if you look back at your emotions and see that feeling of threat, you will see that you made a choice to respond in a racially oppressive way and you need to examine why.

- **Don't force people to acknowledge your good intentions.** What matters is that somebody was hurt. That should be the primary focus. The fact that you hurt someone doesn't mean that you are a horrible person, but the fact that you meant well doesn't absolve you of guilt. Do not make this about your ego. If you truly meant well, then you will continue to mean well and make understanding what just happened your priority.

- **Remember: it's not just this one incident.** This incident is the continuation of a long history of microaggressions for people of color. Racial trauma is cumulative, and you cannot expect a person of color to react to each situation the way that you would having encountered it for the first time. It may not seem fair that you would take some of the blame for what has happened in the past, but what is truly unfair is the fact that people of color have to endure this every day. The privilege you enjoy in not having to constantly suffer these indignities requires that you at least take responsibility for how your actions may be adding to them and the pain that causes.

- **Research further on your own time.** Take whatever knowledge the person confronting you is willing to give gratefully, but do not then demand that they give you a free 101 session on microaggressions. Trust me, whatever it is you've done, it's been done before, and a quick Google search will help you understand further.

- **Apologize.** You've done something that hurt another human being. Even if you don't fully understand why or how, you should apologize. It is the decent thing to do when you respect people. You don't have to totally "get it" to know that you don't want to continue doing something that hurts people.

Talking about microaggressions is hard. It's hard for the person constantly having to bring up the abuses against them, and it's hard for the person constantly feeling like they are doing something wrong. But if you want this to stop—if you want the deluge of little hurts against people of color to stop, if you want the normalization of racism to stop—you have to have these conversations. When it comes to racial oppression, it really is the little things that count.

thirteen

Why are our students so angry?

W HEN MY EIGHT-YEAR-OLD SON IS NERVOUS ABOUT
something, he often moves silently back and forth at
the doorway to my bedroom, where I do most of my writing.
If I don't notice him within a few seconds, he'll very lightly
knock. When he's not nervous, he just bursts right in with no
pretense of manners. We are not usually a house that knocks.
But when he's nervous, he knocks.

That evening, I looked up at the sound of a hesitant little
knock at my doorway and saw the little brown face of my
worried boy.

"Mom?" he said, barely audibly.

I smiled warmly, "Come sit down, baby, tell me what's
up."

My son sat at the end of my bed and fidgeted for a moment
before saying in an almost scared voice, "Mom, I don't want
to go to my assembly at school tomorrow."

My son loves school. He cries at the end of every school year, and jumps for joy at the end of summer. He tries to never miss a single day or any school events.

"Why, baby?" I asked, concerned.

"My music teacher says that if I don't sing the national anthem and say the pledge of allegiance that the veterans will be mad at me," he said, almost in tears.

I was confused for a moment, but then I remembered that Veterans' Day was coming up. "Are veterans coming to your assembly?" I asked.

He nodded, "Yes, and my teacher said that if I don't say the pledge they will walk up to me and yell at me and ask 'why aren't you saying the pledge?' and they'll be hurt because they fought in a war for me and I won't say the pledge for them."

Before I could say anything, my son set his jaw and said, "But I won't say it."

My son had already spent plenty of time explaining to adults why he didn't want to say the pledge of allegiance anymore. He had first told me months earlier, after the same nervous dance at my bedroom door.

"Mom, why do we say the pledge of allegiance at school?"

I was surprised, because even though the recent protests by NFL football quarterback Colin Kaepernick refusing to stand for the national anthem had been all over the news, it was not something I'd discussed with my eight-year-old. Although I'm a very politically active and aware person, I try let my kids be kids and focus when I can on basic intersectional kindness instead of news of complicated public resistance.

But I gave my son a brief history of the pledge of allegiance. He asked a few questions and I answered them (with a Google check or two on my phone). Then he took a deep breath and said, "Mom, I don't think I should say the pledge of allegiance anymore. Would that be okay?"

All activists want their kids to magically turn into badass activists, but I wanted to make sure that this was a decision my son had come to after some thought, and that he had the reasoning to be able to defend that decision. I asked him why he didn't want to say the pledge.

"Because I'm an atheist, so I don't like pledging under god. I don't believe in pledging to countries, I think it encourages war. And I don't think this country treats people who look like me very well so the 'liberty and justice for all' part is a lie. And I don't think that every day we should all be excited about saying a lie."

So when my son came to me the second time, I'd thought we'd worked this pledge business out already. I emailed my son's teacher about his wishes to stop saying the pledge, and the teacher followed up with my son in a supportive conversation and they worked out a compromise. The class recited the pledge of allegiance just like they always did every day and my son respectfully listened but didn't join in. When it was his turn to lead the class in the pledge (kids alternate leading the pledge to teach confidence and leadership skills), he would lead the class in a poem instead. Now, after all of that effort to explain to me and his teacher why he didn't want to say the pledge, he was being required to say it by a different teacher. I was shocked at the thought of any teacher working so hard to intimidate my eight-year-old into compliance, but I looked at my son's face and knew that his mind was made up.

I patted his knee and said, "I don't want you to miss school just because your teacher wanted to scare you. He doesn't understand why you don't want to say the pledge, but that's his problem. You've already explained it to your teachers. No veterans are going to yell at an eight-year-old boy in the middle of an assembly, and if they did, they would be really mean people. But I will make sure that if you go to that assembly and you don't say the pledge and you don't sing the national anthem, nobody will yell at you."

He nodded, went to school, and was silent.

I was once again amazed at how much strength and fight was in this little boy already.

As a parent of a child of color, you try to shield your kids from the harsh realities of the world when you can, while preparing them for the ugliness that they don't have the privilege of being kept safe from. I remember the look of heartbreak on my son's face when our neighbor across the street said that our Black Lives Matter sign was "racist against white people," not knowing that my son had picked it out himself.

Another time, my son told me that his dad had said he could never play with his toy gun from his spy set outside. Best to keep it indoors, he was told.

"Mom, dad said that a boy was playing outside with a toy gun and a cop shot and killed him," he said to me, looking for confirmation of his dad's argument.

That sentence, out of the blue, was like a gut punch. I had spent months trying to not think about the image of twelve-year-old Tamir Rice gunned down at a park by a cop who did not recognize the humanity and childhood of a little boy. A boy who'd been left to die on the ground, while his sister, who ran to help him, was body-slammed and handcuffed.

"That's true," I had to say, "That happened."

"But mom," my son asked, "My stepbrother plays outside with toy guns all the time. How come my dad never told *him* not to?"

I didn't realize it was possible for my heart to break more than it already had. His dad (a white man) had likely never had to consider these possible consequences of toy guns until he saw his little brown boy playing with one, and had to change family rules to accommodate this new reality for him. I had to look at my beautiful son and say, "Well, that's because your stepbrother is white. And cops are more likely to recognize that he's a little boy playing, and that the gun isn't real. I'm so sorry honey. I know it's not fair. Not every cop would think your gun is real, but it's not worth the risk, and your daddy wants to keep you safe."

My son looked at me with tears in his eyes and nodded, then silently walked away.

My son thought about the pledge of allegiance and he looked at this country and he decided that he didn't want to say it anymore.

"I don't think this country treats people who look like me very well so the 'liberty and justice for all' part is a lie. And I don't think that every day we should all be excited about saying a lie."

"Well," I said, "That's a good enough reason for me."

I WAS BORN IN THE '80S, 1980 TO BE EXACT. I GREW UP with the promise of the Cosby family. If you worked hard, you could achieve anything. If you were smart enough, you'd find yourself choosing between Hillman and Yale! Yes, racism still existed and you would occasionally encounter a close-minded fool who would ruin your day with his outdated notions of race. But racism was just that—outdated—and what you would expect, if you played by the rules, was a good life largely unencumbered by the color of your skin.

But the promises of the '80s did not prevent the crack epidemic or the Violent Crime Control and Law Enforcement Act of 1994, which helped militarize our police force, introduced mandatory minimum sentences for crimes more likely to be committed by black and brown offenders, and rapidly expanded prison sizes to accommodate the massive increase of black and brown bodies brought in by a criminal justice system now incentivized to see black and brown people as criminals. The promises of the '80s did not stop the mass incarceration of the 2000's on. The promises of the '80s did not stop families of color from being disproportionately devastated by the housing crisis and the great recession. Even Cosby himself would turn out to be a promise horribly broken. While many in my generation and older had hoped that the election of President Obama would signal some realization of those earlier promises, it is our children who have had to inherit all the ways in which those promises fell short.

We raised our children with the confidence and the audacity to reach for what the promises of the '80s told us our children should be able to achieve. Our parents taught us to strive for the middle-class comfort, safe schools, and steady work that they had fought so very hard for. Because of previous generations, we were able to give our children a freedom that we never had.

And our children took that freedom to high school and college and they realized how little difference our striving has made to the outlook on their futures. We raised our children not knowing that by the time they became adults, one in three black men would be likely to see prison, that they could expect to have one-thirteenth the household income of their white counterparts, that they would see hundreds of black and brown men and women shot and killed by cops every year with no recourse. We raised our kids with all the audacity and hope of generations of protest and progress, and the world expected them to be happy with the sorry state of things as they actually are.

But our kids have seen that, no matter what individual progress we make, no matter how good we strive to be, the system remains. Our kids have seen how every compromise we made over the decades has been turned against them now. Our attempts at respectability have been turned into barriers to recognizing our humanity. Our focus on exceptionalism has been used to justify the murder of the less exceptional. Our focus on allowing "good" people of color to join the ranks of "good" whites has allowed a criminal justice system to swallow up an entire generation deemed "bad."

Our children see how they are allowed in the best colleges, but only if they live in a neighborhood that has enough public school funding to help them get there. Our children see how once they get into that college the curriculum will still teach and promote the history, culture, and politics that keep them oppressed. Our children are seeing their parents lose the homes they worked so hard to afford due to racist lending practices of banks who will never face consequences for their illegal deeds. Our children see how no matter how hard they work, no matter what they accomplish, they could still be in the next viral video as they are gunned down by a cop at a traffic stop. Our children see that, as the world is now, they have nothing to lose.

And our children are remembering how many times we told them that they could do anything. Our children are remembering every time we talked about the civil rights movement and the fight for justice. And they are fighting.

Our children are fighting school systems that teach from racist and colonialist narratives. Our children are fighting the exploitation of student athlete programs. Our children are fighting the language that perpetrates oppression. Our children are fighting to be seen as human beings without any precondition. And our children are fighting for more than just themselves. They have also inherited the vision and accomplishments of disability activists and of Stonewall. Our children believe that justice for people of color includes *all* people of color. And our children are not willing to let anything slide.

Our kids are fighting for a world more just and more righteous than we had ever dared to dream of. The debates we have about gay marriage, transgender bathroom rights, immigration, whether it's "all lives matter" or "black lives matter" have been largely settled in the social world of our youth and they are looking at us dismayed and perplexed at why we just don't get it. In the days after the election of Donald Trump, my older son and a few hundred of his classmates walked out of class and marched to city hall. They were angry and frightened. They had been working so hard to build a better, more inclusive world, and we adults had just royally fucked it up for them. My son sent me video of the protest and I posted it online. Quite a few adults commented: "Shouldn't these kids be learning instead of protesting?" But they had been learning, far more than we apparently had, and that was why they were protesting.

It can be inspiring and also disconcerting to witness our youth in action. They often ask for things that we were brainwashed into believing was "too much to ask for." Trigger warnings? Non-ableist language? Inclusive events? As the newer generation casts us aside it is very easy to find yourself feeling old and . . . wrong. What happens when the youth roll their eyes at principles we've spent our lives fighting for, when they've decided that they are not only outdated, but oppressive?

And this is important to remember, for all of us. No matter what our intentions, everything we say and do in the pursuit of justice will one day be outdated, ineffective, and yes, probably wrong. That is the way progress works. What we do now is important and helpful so long as what we do now is what is needed now. But the arguments I was having in college are not the arguments the world needs now as I prepare to send my son to college. And if I refuse to acknowledge and adjust to that, all I'm doing is making things harder for a generation that would really like to move things forward.

I've learned as a parent that I will never fully agree with or understand my children—especially as they get older. But like I did with my mother, they will find their own way. It is my job as a parent to help give them the platform they need to build their way on, or to smash once they've decided it doesn't work for them. It is my job to keep them safe and support them in the path they choose to take and provide whatever resources I can to that end.

This is the same for our role as the adult generation in society. It is our role not to shape the future, but to not fuck things up so badly that our kids will be too busy correcting the past to focus on the future. It is our job to be confused and dismayed by the future generation, and trust that if we would just stop trying to control them and instead support them, they will eventually find their way.

My goal as a writer and an activist is not to shape future generations. I hope to give a platform, a foundation for our young people to build upon and then smash to bits when it is no longer needed. That is what our kids are doing right now, with all of the work we have done, all that we have dedicated to them—they are building upon it so that they can smash it all down. And it's a beautiful thing to see.

fourteen

What is the model minority myth?

I SPENT MY ENTIRE CHILDHOOD AND THE ENTIRETY OF my twenties poor. No, not momentarily broke where you can't go to the concert you want or can't eat out for dinner that week—I mean *poor*. The type of poor that cuts the electricity off, that doesn't have a phone, that eats dinners in soup kitchens. I remember trying to sleep longer so that I would have less time awake to feel hungry. I remember sneaking down the hall to use a vacant apartment to shower after our water had been cut off. But I also remember that we weren't alone.

We certainly were not the only poor kids, although in our neighborhood, we were perhaps a bit poorer than most. But there were poor black kids and poor brown kids, and occasionally some poor white kids. I would gravitate to other brown and black kids in my neighborhood naturally, not because I assumed that we'd have a deep connection racially, but because I felt like we'd be more likely to have a connection economically—which for kids, can matter more than just about everything. Yes, I'd been mocked for my dark skin and coarse hair, but I'd been mocked far more for the mustard sandwiches I brought for lunch, the oil lamps and candles we often used to light our apartment, or the fact that nobody could call me on the phone.

Chances were, if you were brown, and you lived in my apartment complex, you were almost as poor as me. And you could spend the night at my house and we'd scrounge up a dollar for some packages of ramen and if the power went out we'd crumble up the dry noodles and eat them like chips under candlelight and nobody would think that it was weird or shameful.

I had friends you could go to the food bank with. Friends who wouldn't be embarrassed if you paid for your groceries with food stamps. I had friends that never expected fancy gifts. I had friends who never looked at the label on your clothes because ours all had said Goodwill on paper tags when we got them. I had friends who never asked where your mom was because we all knew our moms were working. And because we were all poor, none of us ever had any material thing to be jealous over or petty about. We were just kids, and for the most part, we were happy.

This isn't to say that being poor was just fine—it wasn't. We still felt every bit of shame that the outside world wanted to pile upon us. We still saw the worried looks on our parents' faces as they tried to figure out how they were going to make $20 last a week and a half. We still saw how much less our teachers expected from us. But when we were together, we could pretend, even for a little while, that we were the normal ones. That we weren't broken.

I didn't realize until I was an adult that most of my poor childhood friends were Asian American or Pacific Islanders. My idea of Asian Americans very much fit in with the popular stereotype of hard-working, financially and academically successful, quiet, serious people of predominantly East Asian (Chinese, Korean, or Japanese) descent. But most of my friends' parents were from Guam, the Philippines, Vietnam, Cambodia, Laos, and India. Most of my friends' parents had fled war, conflict, and economic disaster. They were all poor, they were all struggling, and they were all discriminated against for their brown skin and their strong accents. But even though they were my friends, their racial and ethnic identity was invisible to me and continued to be so well into my adulthood.

And so when I started fighting for racial equality they were not on my mind. When I started fighting for economic justice, they were not on my mind. And still today, even after having spent years of my life focused on racial justice, Asian Americans are at times an afterthought in my work.

I'm not proud to admit it, but it's the truth. This is not because I do not know and love many Asian American people—but that excuse doesn't work for me any more than it does for anybody else. It's because I'm a product of this country and I'm just as susceptible to the narrative that fetishizes and erases Asian Americans as anybody else. I, like so many of us, have to do better.

When we think about race in America most of us (with the notable exception of many Asian Americans) think in terms of black and white, and maybe brown Latinx and white, and maybe—just maybe—American Indians and white. But we rarely talk about the model minority myth and how it affects Asian Americans. And if we do talk about it, we rarely talk about it as a problem.

The model minority myth fetishizes Asian Americans—reducing a broad swath of the world's population to a simple stereotype. The model minority myth places undue burdens and expectations on Asian American youth and erases any who struggle to live up to them. The model minority myth erases religious minorities, it erases refugees, it erases queer Asian Americans. The model minority myth gives a pretty blanket for society to hide its racism against Asian Americans under, while separating them from other people of color who suffer from the same white supremacist system. The model minority myth is active racism that is harming Asian Americans, and we need to talk about it.

SOMETHING CALLED "MODEL MINORITY" DOESN'T SEEM like it would be a problem. When we think of being a "model" for a group, we think of being someone to aspire to. For many people in the Asian American and Pacific Islander (AAPI) community who complain about the model minority myth, this argument, that being a "model minority" is not actually something to complain about, is often used to silence them. These complaints are often met with an overly simplistic idea of what the model minority myth is. But no, the problem isn't actually that society just sees Asian Americans as "just too great." It isn't that Asian Americans are "just too successful." The model minority myth is much more complicated and harmful than that.

What is the model minority myth?

Originally coined in 1966 by sociologist William Peterson to profile the socioeconomic success of Japanese Americans, the myth of the "model minority" has become a collection of stereotypes about Asian Americans, presenting them as an "ideal minority group" in the eyes of White Supremacy. Included in these stereotypes are presumptions of academic and financial success, social and political meekness, a strong work ethic, dominance in math and the sciences, and strict parenting. Peterson's use of "model minority" was to study the success of Asian Americans, contrasting them with what he termed "problem minorities."

While some in the Asian American community embraced these stereotypes, many others fought against it. The work of Asian American scholars like Bob Suzuki's "Education and the Socialization of Asian Americans: A Revisionist Analysis of the 'Model Minority' Thesis" and Ki-Taek Chun's "The Myth of Asian American Success and Its Educational Ramifications" helped lead early pushback against the idea that all Asian Americans were destined to succeed.

On the surface, the model minority myth does not seem like a myth. Asian Americans do have some of the highest rates of college graduation, highest salaries, and lowest incarceration rates of minority groups in America. But Asian American sociologists, psychologists, educators, and activists have helped shed light on the reality of life for Asian Americans that the model minority myth hides, and the real harm that it does.

When we say "Asian American" we are talking about an incredibly broad swath of cultures and histories representing a very large portion of the globe. When we say "Asian American" we are talking about not just people of Japanese,

Korean, and Chinese descent, but also South Asians, Southeast Asians, Pacific Islanders, Indian Americans, Hmong Americans, Vietnamese Americans, Samoans, Native Hawaiians, and more. When we say "Asian American" we are talking about war refugees, tech professionals who first arrived on H-1B visas, and third-generation Midwesterners. When we say "Asian American" we are talking about so much more than can be fit in a single stereotype.

While every racial minority in the US is subject to harmful stereotyping, the model minority myth becomes hard to combat when it is not seen as harmful because the people most harmed by it are also made invisible by it. So who and what do we not see when we see the "model minority?" Quite a lot:

- **Pacific Islanders.** The culture, history, and voices of people of Hawaiian, Guamanian, Tongan, Fijian, Samoan, and Marshallese descent, and more, are largely invisible to greater American society and culture, and the needs of Pacific Islanders are often left out of discussions on the needs of Asian Americans.

- **Extreme economic disparity**. While as a whole, Asian Americans have wealth and poverty rates similar to those of white Americans, that statistic covers up a wide disparity of wealth and poverty amongst Asian Americans when you look at country of origin. Filipino Americans, on average, have a low poverty rate of 6.7 percent—more than 3 percentage points lower than white Americans. But Cambodian, Laotian, Pakistani, and Thai Americans have a poverty rate of around 18 percent. Bangladeshi and Hmong Americans have poverty rates between 26 and 28

percent, matching or surpassing that of blacks and Hispanic Americans.[1] Pacific Islanders have the highest un-
employment rate of any racial or ethnic group in the US.[2]
As Ronald Takaki pointed out in his book *A Different
Mirror: A History of Multicultural America*, a fair amount
of this economic disparity can be attributed to how Asian
Americans immigrated to America over time. Asian Americans were first derided as "unskilled labor" until the 1965
Immigration Act prioritized Asian Americans who were
more highly educated and financially successful, in the belief that they would "contribute" more to American society. As the most privileged and skilled immigrants from
China and Japan entered the US, the stereotype of Asian
Americans in the US changed to one of a cultural incli-
nation for academic and business success—ignoring the
fact that the majority of Chinese and Japanese people who
were unable to immigrate did not enjoy the same high
levels of income or education. As that myth took hold, it
did not adjust to accommodate the vastly different social,
educational, and economic circumstances that Asian refugees were coming from as they fled countries like Vietnam
and Cambodia. Nor did it account for the social and economic barriers they, like many other refugee populations,
would face when they arrived in the US.

- **Extreme educational disparity.** While in 2013 Asian
  Americans had the highest college graduation rate of any
  racial group in America by far with 53 percent, as with
  overall numbers of economic success, this number hides
  a wide disparity based on country of origin: 46 percent
  of second-generation Cambodian and Laotian Americans

have only a high school degree or less, compared to only 6 percent of second-generation Chinese Americans. The model minority myth makes it even harder for struggling Asian American students to find academic success, as studies have shown that it causes many K–12 educators to believe that Asian American students need less academic resources for their success—even though approximately one in three Asian Americans (especially those raised in households where English is not spoken) lack proficiency in writing, reading, and speaking skills.[3] And while many Asian Americans suffer these economic disadvantages and lack of resources, they often face lower acceptance rates to colleges and universities because they are seen as "overrepresented" in US higher education. When you add in the US immigration processes encouraging a "brain drain" of elites from countries like China and India, the vast majority of the "academic success" we see when we think of Asian Americans is only available to wealthy, highly skilled immigrants who already have a high level of education, and their offspring—while only 17 percent of Pacific Islanders, 14 percent of Cambodian Americans, and 13 percent of Laotian and Hmong Americans have four-year college degrees,[4] compared to 22 percent of black Americans and 15 percent of Hispanic Americans.[5] The stereotype that Asian Americans naturally excel at math and science also discourages Asian American students from pursuing careers in the arts and humanities and keeps those who do pursue those careers from being taken seriously in their fields. A 2009 census report showed that under 15 percent of Asian American degree holders majored in the arts and humanities, less than any other racial or ethnic group in America.[6]

- **Limits on professional success.** While Asian Americans are seen as professional success stories, very few are able to make it the top of their fields, despite the education and qualifications that they are known for. A 2011 study showed that Asian Americans made up only 1.4 percent of Fortune 500 CEOs and 1.9 percent of all corporate officer positions, and 63 percent of Asian American men reported feeling "stalled" in their careers.[7] While Asian Americans make up between 35 and 60 percent of the workforce in top tech companies like Google and Facebook, they are less than half as likely to reach management levels in the tech industry as their white counterparts.[8]

- **Hate crimes against Asian Americans.** Hate crimes against all Asian American groups are given little attention in the United States, but because the model minority myth focuses so heavily on East Asians as the definition of Asian Americans, the alarming rise of hate crimes against South Asians is often ignored. General cultural ignorance about many South Asians makes them targets for violent Islamophobia, even if they are not Muslim. Since the terror attacks on September 11, 2001, many Sikhs and Hindus have reported being the victims of hate attacks by those mistaking them for Muslim Americans. In the first month after the attack, three hundred hate crimes against Sikh Americans were documented by The Sikh Coalition. In the San Francisco Bay area, 69 percent of turban-wearing Sikh students reported harassment or bullying in a 2008 survey.[9] In 2012 a white supremacist opened fire in a Sikh temple in Wisconsin, killing six and wounding four.

- **Health and safety of Asian American women.** The stereotype of the docile and subservient Asian woman is often used to encourage and hide abuse of Asian women by their partners. Between 41 and 61 percent of Asian American women will be physically or sexually abused by their partners in their lifetime—twice the national average for all women.[10] Studies also show higher rates of depression and suicidal thoughts in Asian American women. Yet Asian American women are rarely the focus of domestic violence awareness, victim advocacy, or mental health efforts.

- **Lack of political power.** The stereotype of the "meek" Asian American, combined with social pressure to stick to science and technology fields, has discouraged many Asian Americans from seeking political leadership and activism roles and prevents those who do seek those roles from being seen as "strong enough" leaders for the task. As of 2017 there is only one Asian American in the US Senate, and only eleven Asian Americans in the House of Representatives. There has not been an Asian American president or vice president in the US, and there have only been seven Asian American state governors in US history so far.

- **Everyday discrimination and microaggressions against Asian Americans.** The model minority myth puts a lot of pressure on Asian Americans to seem happy with their "great success" in America and live up to the hard-working and docile image projected onto them. This makes it very hard for Asian Americans to complain about racist microaggressions against them, and makes it even harder for them to be taken seriously when they do.

- **Common struggle with other people of color.** "Why can't you be like the Asians? They come here with nothing and work hard and make themselves into a great success. You aren't oppressed, you're just lazy." This is a common refrain that many non-Asian people of color hear from white people when they try to address systemic racism in America. The model minority myth is often used to separate Asian Americans from other people of color by using their perceived socioeconomic and academic success and docile nature to compare and contrast with black Americans, Hispanic Americans, and Native Americans. This divide-and-conquer technique serves to redirect struggle against oppressive White Supremacy to competition between Asian Americans and other people of color. The real animosity between some Asian Americans and other people of color that has been manufactured by the model minority myth prevents Asian Americans and non-Asian people of color from recognizing and organizing around shared experiences of labor exploitation, lack of government representation, lack of pop culture representation, cultural appropriation, and much more.

This is just a small sample of the many ways in which the racist model minority myth harms Asian Americans. The model minority myth is not a myth designed to benefit Asian Americans, it was designed to benefit White Supremacy through the exploitation of Asian American labor, the neglect of poor and disenfranchised Asian Americans, the exotification of Asian American culture, the exclusion of Asian Americans from systems of power, the sexual exploitation of Asian American women, and the comparison of the model minority status of Asian Americans to other racial minorities in order to delegitimize the claims of oppression and the struggles of black and Hispanic Americans.

If you want to fight racism in America, you have to fight the model minority myth. Far too often, this wide-reaching form of racism is left out of our discussions on issues of racial oppression and discrimination. Far too often our Asian American friends and neighbors are not offered a seat at the equality and anti-racism table, and far too often their own efforts at combating anti-Asian racism are ignored by the broader social justice community. Non-Asians must try to prioritize Asian American issues and voices just as we should prioritize the issues and voices of other racial minorities in not only our social justice efforts, but also our government, our board rooms, and our film and television screens. We must be willing to listen and learn when we are called out for our anti-Asian microaggressions and our complicity in the model minority myth. We must be willing to fight the white supremacist narrative designed to divide Asian Americans from other racial and ethnic groups in the US and to fight for their freedom and equality as we do our own. And finally, Asian and non-Asian people of color must stop believing the hype: we are not in competition for the biggest slice of the white supremacist pie. We will never be free until we are all seen and valued for our unique culture, history, talents, and challenges. We cannot win this battle against racism if we do not realize that there is no set of racial or ethnic stereotypes that will set us free, no matter how appealing they seem on the surface.

fifteen

But what if I hate Al Sharpton?

WHEN I WAS A KID I LIKED MARTIN LUTHER KING Jr. and I did not like Malcolm X. Those two thoughts were always linked for me. There were two sides to the fight for racial justice: MLK was on one, Malcolm was on the other. Malcolm and Martin had always been presented in this dichotomy to me and to many other Americans. Martin was on the side of love and equality; Malcolm was on the side of anger and separation.

This was taught in school and in popular culture and even at home. "Martin Luther King wanted a world without color" people would also say. "Malcolm X hated white people," they would also say. We learned all about Martin Luther King, the pacifist who loved America into racial harmony. We heard cherry-picked segments of his speeches, talking about little black and white children living in peace. We saw King walk side by side with white people on the path to a post-race America.

Malcolm we saw as the cautionary tale, what could happen if you let your bitterness at racial oppression get to you. We saw Malcolm as a man corrupted by hate that made him no better than his oppressors. Whereas Martin's death was seen as the martyrdom of a legend, Malcolm's death was no more than a natural consequence of being black and angry.

This same Martin/Malcolm dichotomy is applied to all people of color, and especially black people, who fight for racial justice. A few of us are good and worthy of support. Those of us who manage to say "not all white people" enough, who manage to say please, who never talk of anger, who avoid words like "justice," who keep our indictments abstract and never specific—we are the Martins. Those of us who shout, who inconvenience your day, who call out your specific behavior, who say "black" loudly and proudly—we are the Malcolms.

And while the image of Malcolm X has been swapped out for the image of Al Sharpton, or Jesse Jackson, the impact of being labeled as such is the same—you are not worthy of support, your cause is corrupt, you are why people will not fight for you.

This is a message I receive on a regular basis. I receive Facebook comments, Twitter DMs, and emails telling me that "people like me" are the reason why race relations are as bad as they are. My insistence on voicing my anger, on using terms like "White Supremacy" and "racist" to define White Supremacy and things that are racist, my insistence on being seen and acknowledged as black—that is the real issue. White people would love to join me in my fight for freedom and justice, but I've made it too unpleasant for them.

These comments used to sting, they used to take me aback. They called to all of the messaging that I and so many other black people had been inundated with their entire lives—there are black people who deserve equality, and black people who don't—and if you don't, you have nobody to blame but yourself. I would second-guess myself, check my language, quiet my voice. But a quieter, gentler voice did not bring a quieter, gentler world. All it did was give people the impression that I was okay with living like a second-class citizen. All it did was increase my burden.

But here's the thing: Martin Luther King was not the "MLK" of his time, not the "MLK" of legend. Martin Luther King was public enemy number one. Seen as an even greater threat by our government, and a large portion of society, than Malcolm X was. Because what Martin Luther King Jr and Malcolm X fought for was the same: freedom from oppression. At times they used different words and different tactics, but it was their goal that was the threat. Their goal of freedom from racial oppression was and is a direct threat to the system of White Supremacy. And for all of Martin's actions of peace and love, he was targeted with violence, harassed, arrested, blackmailed, followed by the FBI, and eventually murdered. For all of the pedestals MLK is now put on, far above the reach of ordinary black Americans, Martin was in his life viewed as the most dangerous man in America. Martin was the black man who asked for too much, too loudly. Martin was why white America couldn't support equality. Because no matter what we ask for, if it threatens the system of White Supremacy, it will always be seen as too much.

When we were slaves nursing their babies, we were not nice enough. When we were maids cleaning their homes we were not nice enough. When we were porters shining their shoes we were not nice enough. And when we danced and sang for their entertainment we were not nice enough.

For hundreds of years we have been told that the path to freedom from racial oppression lies in our virtue, that our humanity must be earned. We simply don't *deserve* equality yet.

So when people say that they don't like my tone, or when they say they can't support the "militancy" of Black Lives Matter, or when they say that it would be easier if we just didn't talk about race all the time—I ask one question:

Do you believe in justice and equality?

Because if you believe in justice and equality you believe in it all of the time, for all people. You believe in it for newborn babies, you believe in it for single mothers, you believe in it for kids in the street, you believe in justice and equality for people you like and people you don't. You believe in it for people who don't say please.

And if there was anything I could say or do that would convince someone that I or people like me don't deserve justice or equality, then they never believed in justice and equality in the first place.

Yes, I am a Malcolm. And Martin, and Angela, Marcus, Rosa, Biko, Baldwin, Assata, Harriet, and Nina. I'm fighting for liberation. I'm filled with righteous anger and love. I'm shouting, as all before me have in their way. And I'm a human being who was born deserving justice and equality, and that is all you should need to know in order to stand by my side.

"WE WILL NEVER GET ANYWHERE IF YOU ARE GOING TO resort to insults."

"This is why nobody wants to help you."

"If you want white people to help you, you should be nicer to them."

"Why are they so angry? It makes it hard for people to support them."

Let's talk about tone policing. If you've had conversations about social justice on the Internet you've likely heard this term. When I talk about tone policing with people online or in person, I find that many people don't fully understand what it means, they just know that it's not something they want to be accused of.

Maybe tone policing is something you've been accused of yourself. You were having a conversation about race and things started to get heated. You were just trying to keep things calm and civil and BAM!—you've been found guilty of "tone policing."

You've been found guilty, and you aren't quite sure how, but suddenly you have been deemed "the problem." What gives?

"Tone policing" is an important term to understand if you want to have productive conversations about race and if you have been tone policing, you've been doing something harmful—whether you mean to or not.

So what is tone policing? Tone policing is when someone (usually the privileged person) in a conversation or situation about oppression shifts the focus of the conversation from the oppression being discussed to the *way* it is being discussed. Tone policing prioritizes the comfort of the privileged person in the situation over the oppression of the disadvantaged person. This is something that can happen in a conversation, but can also apply to critiques of entire civil rights organizations and movements.

Most damagingly, tone policing places prerequisites on being heard and being helped.

You may be reading the above and thinking, "well, that sounds like a healthy way to avoid stressful and harmful conversations. Isn't that how we're taught to handle people who are treating us with disrespect? Aren't we supposed to stand up for ourselves if people are being mean or rude?" First, let me be clear that accusations of tone policing don't apply to actual abuse—threats and violence are not okay. Neither is bringing more oppression into the conversation as a weapon against oppressors (say, using ableist slurs in response to racism). But hurt feelings and rudeness are not oppression, and will always come second to the oppression being discussed. For a simple disagreement about, say, who should take the garbage out, it would be reasonable to insist that people don't start shouting. But conversations on race and systemic oppression are never that simple.

This isn't your typical household or workplace argument. No discussion about racism is just about one incident for people of color, because we cannot divorce ourselves from the past pain of systemic racism, or the future repercussions of current abuse. When people of color talk about systemic racism, far more than feelings have been hurt and far more than feelings are at stake. When people of color are talking about racism, no matter the immediate subject, they are also always talking about lifelong abuse at the hands of society.

When I talk about police brutality, I am talking about the pain of seeing black men and women shot like dogs in the street, the fear for myself and my brothers and sons, the rage that we won't see justice. When you talk about oppression with oppressed people, you are talking with hurt, scared, angry, and grieving people.

If you've been privileged enough to not suffer from the cumulative effects of systemic racism and are therefore able to look at racially charged situations one at a time, and then let it go, please recognize that very few people of color are able to enter into discussions on racism with the same freedom.

When people of color speak out about systemic racism, they are opening up all of that pain and fear and anger to you. They are not doing this because they enjoy it; it is an incredibly painful and vulnerable experience. We do this because we have to, because systemic racism is killing us. And yes, that pain and fear and anger will sometimes show in our words and our actions. But to see all that pain, and how we fight still after entire lifetimes of struggle—and then to tell us to be more polite is just plain cruel.

To refuse to listen to someone's cries for justice and equality until the request comes in a language you feel comfortable with is a way of asserting your dominance over them in the situation. The oppressed person reaching out to you is already disadvantaged by the oppression they are trying to address. By tone policing, you are increasing that disadvantage by insisting that you get to determine if their grievances are valid and will only decide they are so if, on top of everything they are already enduring, they make the effort to prioritize your comfort. Whether you are consciously meaning to do this or not, this is the effect tone policing has on people of color.

There will always be people within movements that you do not like. There will always be actions that people within movements take that you will not agree with. And you certainly do not have to blindly follow a movement just because you believe in the cause—in fact, it's very important that you always keep your eyes open and stay true to your morals.

But do not let your feelings about a person within the movement become the focus of your work toward fighting racial oppression. Even if you do not agree with the way in which someone is going about their fight for racial justice, recognize when they are indeed fighting for it, and that you do have the same goals. When you instead shift your focus to getting people of color to fight oppression in a way in which you approve, racial justice is no longer your main goal—your approval is. Find areas of the movement for equality with which you feel confident that the main goal is equality and within which you do not feel that you are violating your principles. Do work there, and where that work coincides with the work of others, join hands. Remember, this isn't about you, and it isn't about the person in the movement that you do not like.

Work will be, and constantly is, done within movements to make them more effective. Critique already exists from within, rest assured. Movements grow and change. Do not think that there is a complaint against a member of the racial justice movement that you could lodge that has not already being debated. But know that if you are a privileged person trying to impose your wishes on social justice movements, you are trying to remake that movement in your image, which is exactly what social justice movements are fighting against.

IF YOU ARE A WHITE PERSON CONCERNED WITH FIGHTing racial oppression, and you want to avoid this sort of tone policing behavior and stay focused on being a true ally in the battle against racism, here are some things to remember:

- **Be aware of the limits of your empathy.** Your privilege will keep you from fully understanding the pain caused to people of color by systemic racism, but just because you cannot understand it, that does not make it any less real.
- **Don't distract or deflect.** The core issue in discussions of racism and systemic oppression will always be racism and systemic oppression.
- **Remember your goal.** Your main goal, if you consider yourself an ally, should always be to end systemic racism.
- **Drop the prerequisites.** That goal should not have any preconditions on it. You are fighting systemic racism because it is your moral obligation, and that obligation is yours as long as systemic racism exists, pure and simple.
- **Walk away if you must, but don't give up.** If you simply cannot abide an oppressed person or group's language or methods, step aside and find where you can help elsewhere.
- **Build a tolerance for discomfort.** You must get used to being uncomfortable and get used to this not being about your feelings if you plan to help and not hinder people of color in their efforts for racial justice.

- **You are not doing any favors, you are doing what is right.** If you are white, remember that White Supremacy is a system you benefit from and that your privilege has helped to uphold. Your efforts to dismantle White Supremacy are expected of decent people who believe in justice. You are not owed gratitude or friendship from people of color for your efforts. We are not thanked for cleaning our own houses.

If you are a person of color who is being shamed or criticized by privileged people for your tone, please remember this:

- **You have a right to your anger, sadness and fear.** These are natural reactions to the unnatural system of racial oppression.
- **You were born deserving equality and justice.** Nobody should be able to take that away from you. Your humanity does not have to be earned.
- **You matter.** You are no less important than those who try to put preconditions on your humanity.
- **Nobody has authority over your fight for racial justice.** Those who tone-police you are trying to manipulate you into thinking that their validation is required to legitimize your desire for racial justice. This is abusive behavior.
- **You deserve to be able to speak your truth, and you deserve to be heard.**

Conversations about race and racial oppression can certainly be tough, but that's nothing compared to how tough fighting against racial oppression can be. Our humanity is worth a little discomfort, it's actually worth a *lot* of discomfort. But if you live in this system of White Supremacy you are either fighting the system, or you are complicit. There is no neutrality to be had towards systems of injustice—it is not something you can just opt out of. If you believe in justice and equality, we are in this together, whether you like me or not.

sixteen

I just got called racist, what do I do now?

"IT WAS ONE OF THE MOST DISGUSTING MOMENTS OF my presidency," George W. Bush declared earnestly to Matt Lauer.[1] Two years after his presidency, during which he started two wars that cost hundreds of thousands of lives and destabilized an entire region of the world, the former president was talking about the moments that had stood out to him. And there, in his list of "the most disgusting moments" was the time that Kanye West said that George W. Bush doesn't care about black people.

In his book *Decision Points*, Bush talks further about how hurt he was by Kanye's accusation. It was, in his words, an all-time low of his presidency: "I faced a lot of criticism as president. I didn't like hearing people claim that I lied about Iraq's weapons of mass destruction or cut taxes to benefit the rich.

But the suggestion that I was racist because of the response to Katrina represented an all-time low."

I remember at the time feeling shocked and a little amused by this. After all the atrocities that George W. Bush saw in his presidency (terror attacks, unjust wars resulting in hundreds of thousands of deaths, the largest recession since the great depression, and so much more) having someone insinuate that he was racist was the all-time low. How out-of-touch. How self-centered. I remember thinking that it was yet another sign that the former president was a weird emotional child who was not at all qualified for the presidency (this was, of course, before Donald Trump showed us all what "weird, emotional child not at all qualified for the presidency" really looks like). But I thought of this mostly as a funny aberration.

That was, of course, until I started writing about race.

If you write about race or talk about race, you will quickly realize that GWB's reaction to the insinuation of racism is disturbingly common. To many white people, it appears, there is absolutely nothing worse than being called a racist, or someone insinuating you might be racist, or someone saying that something you did was racist, or somebody calling somebody you identify with racist. Basically, anytime the label of racist touches you at all, it's the worst thing to happen to anybody anywhere.

I remember once after sharing an article on Twitter about racism in the US, when a white Canadian tweeted back, "You should move to Canada, we aren't racist here." I pointed out that, according to recent news of the reluctance of government officials to fully investigate the murders of dozens of indigenous women, the controversy over "carding" of black

Canadians by police, and the testimony of my Canadian friends of color—Canada was plenty racist. This white Canadian stranger kept insisting that no, there was no racism in Canada because he had not seen it. When some of my Canadian friends chimed in with helpful links about high-profile incidences of racism and investigations into systemic racism in Canada, the white Canadian continued to insist that they were wrong, and that racism doesn't exist in Canada.

I pointed out the irony of stating that racism doesn't exist, while talking over, belittling, and denying the lived experiences of Canadians of color.

His response was quick: "Are you calling me racist? YOU CUNT."

Mr. Friendly White Canadian then proceeded to harass me on social media for weeks, until his account was suspended. For hours each day he sought out anyone who commented on one of my Tweets, informing them that I was a "reverse-racist" who "hated white people" and "loved calling innocent people racists." After I blocked him on Twitter, he would log on from other accounts he created just to continue the harassment. He did not appear to be, from his Internet history, a professional troll or serial harasser. Something about my insinuation that his actions may be racist had triggered a deep rage inside of him, and he was going to make me pay.

This is perhaps a slightly more extreme example of the racial confrontation formula: a white person does something racially insensitive and harmful, it is pointed out to them, and they go nuclear. People have tried to get me fired from gigs, have tried to organize protests of my public events, have sent me threatening emails—all for pointing out how their actions are hurting others.

And I'm not alone. When I asked a group of people of color what they feared most when talking about racism, their number-one concern was retaliation. One friend knows of at least two websites dedicated to smearing her because she called a white woman's language racist. One friend was fired from a job after a Facebook argument in which she said an associate was acting racist. One friend was subject to a months-long campaign to turn her community against her after stating that someone's actions were insensitive to people of color. Countless friends have had emails sent to their employers and educators by white people incensed that someone would insinuate that their actions are racist.

Even when the words "racist" or "racism" are never said—even the slightest implication can shift the entire conversation from "Hey, this hurts people of color" to "DID YOU JUST CALL ME RACIST? I AM NOT RACIST! I AM A GOOD PERSON HOW DARE YOU?"

It's not as if it's easy for people of color to call out racism. When we decide to talk about these things, not only are we having to confront our own feelings of hurt, disappointment, or anger, we know that we are also risking any of the above reactions and more. When we decide to talk about racism, we know that it could indeed end our friendships, our reputations, our careers, and even our lives. The response to our complaints of racism or racial insensitivity are not always met with such violent reactions, but no matter what, it is never a pleasant conversation for people of color to have. I do not know a single person of color who does not broach these conversations with a very heavy heart, and they almost always leave with one even heavier.

So why do we talk about racism if it's so risky and so painful?

Because we have no choice. Because not talking about it is killing us. Because for far too long, the burden of racism has always been on us alone. If you are white, and you are reading this and wondering why we bother if these conversations are as bad as I say, think of how bad the alternative—continued, unchecked racism—would have to be in order to get you to risk that much, and you'll know a little more about the reality of life for people of color.

THIS CHAPTER IS FOR WHITE PEOPLE. OF COURSE, NON-white people will read it as well, and I hope that it is informative to most and perhaps validating to others. But I am aiming this chapter at you, the white person who is afraid of being called racist. Who may well be avoiding further investing in the fight for racial justice because you know that one wrong move may have you labeled as a white supremacist. If you see even a little bit of yourself in this, you need to keep reading. If you are convinced that you are past all of that, you should probably still keep reading—because these defensive impulses run deep and may take you by surprise, just when you thought you had gotten past all of your discomfort around race.

Who are you?

You are, at times, kind and mean, generous and selfish, witty and dull. Sometimes you are all of these things at once.

And if you are white in a white supremacist society, you are racist. If you are male in a patriarchy, you are sexist. If you are able-bodied, you are ableist. If you are anything above poverty in a capitalist society, you are classist. You can sometimes be all of these things at once.

You do, as Walt Whitman said, contain multitudes.

I know that the above is all that some people need to chuck this book out a window. "Typical," some might say, "Another Social Justice Warrior who thinks all white people are racist." But you've come this far and already invested so much in this process—please, consider sitting with your discomfort for a while longer, and see where this chapter takes you.

We like to think of our character in the same way it is written in our obituaries. We are strong, brave, and loyal. We are funny and creative. We are what we strive to be. While if we sit and reflect, we can provide a more nuanced description of ourselves, in our day-to-day lives our self-esteem reads in synopsis: "Mary was a kind and loving mother. An avid gardener."

But life is a series of moments. And in reality we are both the culmination of those countless moments, and each moment individually in time.

Say you get drunk in a bar and punch a stranger in the face, spend the night in jail, realize that your life has taken a turn for the worse, get treatment, stop drinking, and dedicate your life to anti-violence work. To the person that you punched that night, you may forever be the person who assaulted them. The person who made them scared to go into bars for a while. The person who made them feel violated. To the people you have helped since, you may always be a hero. The person who made them safer in the world.

These are both who you are, they are both valid and do not cancel each other out. If you run into the person you punched years later, they may well still be afraid of you, they may react with anger. They will treat you like someone who punched them, because you are. And even if you respond to that anger and fear like someone who abhors violence, because that is also who you are, you have no right to demand that they see you differently.

Why all of this talk about the ways in which we can all be both an abuser and a healer? Because you have been racist, and you have been anti-racist. Yes, you may now be insisting that you do not have a racist bone in your body, but that is simply not true. You have been racist, and will be in the future, even if less so.

You are racist because you were born and bred in a racist, white supremacist society. White Supremacy is, as I've said earlier, insidious by design. The racism required to uphold White Supremacy is woven into every area of our lives. There is no way you can inherit white privilege from birth, learn racist white supremacist history in schools, consume racist and white supremacist movies and films, work in a racist and white supremacist workforce, and vote for racist and white supremacist governments and not be racist.

This does not mean that you have hate in your heart. You may intend to treat everyone equally. But it does mean that you have absorbed some fucked-up shit regarding race, and it will show itself in some fucked-up ways. You may not know why you clutch your purse a little harder when a black man walks by you, but in the moment you do, you are being racist. You may not know why when you see a bad driver on the road and you recognize they are Asian a little voice inside you goes "Aha!" but in that moment, you are being racist. You may not know why you are pleasantly surprised that the Latinx person you are talking to is "so articulate" but in that moment, you are being racist.

And that racism informs a lot of your decisions in ways that you are not aware. It informs how you vote, where you spend your money, whom you hire, what books you read, whom you socialize with, what social concerns you will pay attention to. And that racism does real harm to real people, both immediately and systematically. To the person you harmed in that racist moment, you may forever be the person who harmed them, because you did. You may also be other things to them—you may also be a friend, a coworker, or a neighbor. And you can decide that you don't ever want to be a racist to anyone else, and you can work toward that goal, but you cannot tell someone to deny the harm you've done to them.

And that sucks. It sucks to know that to some people you will forever be the person who harmed them. It sucks to know that someone you have harmed in the past may one day read in your obituary "John was a generous and loyal friend to all he met" and disagree. You've tried so hard to be a good person, but your intentions cannot erase the harm that your actions cause.

This is real harm that has been done and you have to accept that if you do not want to continue harming people by denying their lived experiences and denying your responsibility. This does not mean that you have to flog yourself for all eternity. The pain you've caused is real, and if you have a conscience, the recognition of that will likely sting a little whenever you think about it. But everything else you've done, all of the effort you've made to be a better person, that is just as valid and deserves equal billing in your obit. Your mistakes or your achievements will never on their own define you. But you can only do better if you are willing to look at your entire self.

All of this is to say that if you have been called racist, or something you have done has been called racist, by a person of color, you cannot simply dismiss it outright—even if that accusation is in direct opposition to all that you try to be. Not if you are truly committed to racial justice.

Now is an opportunity to learn more about yourself, to see yourself and your actions more clearly, so you can move toward the person you truly want to be. The question is: do you want to *look* like a better person, or do you want to *be* a better person? Because those who just want to look like a better person will have great difficulty with the introspection necessary to actually be a better person. In order to do better we must be willing to hold our darkness to the light, we must be willing to shatter our own veneer of "goodness"

So if you've been confronted with the possibility of your own racism, and you want to *do the work*, here are some tips:

- **Listen.** First and foremost, if someone is telling you something about yourself and your actions and you feel your hackles raising, take that as a sign that you need to stop and listen. If your blood pressure rose too quickly to really hear what was being said, take a few deep breaths, ask the person to repeat themselves if necessary, and listen again. Don't add to what the person is saying, don't jump to conclusions, don't immediately think "Oh you think I'm a monster now," just try to actually hear what they are trying to communicate to you.

- **Set your intentions aside.** Your intentions have little to no impact on the way in which your actions may have harmed others. Do not try to absolve yourself of responsibility with your good intentions.

- **Try to hear the impact of what you have done.** Don't just hear the action: "You consistently speak over me in work meetings and you do not do that to white people in our meetings." That is easy to brush off as, "I just didn't agree with you," or, "I didn't mean to, I was just excited about a point I was trying to make. Don't make a big deal out of nothing." Try to also hear the impact: "You bias is invalidating my professional expertise and making me feel singled out and unappreciated in a way which compounds all of the many ways I'm made to feel this way as a woman of color in the workplace."

- **Remember that you do not have all of the pieces.** You are not living as a person of color. You will never fully understand the impact that sustained, systemic racism has on people of color. You will never be able to fully empathize with the pain your actions may have caused. Nothing will get you there. Do not discount someone's complaint because their emotions seem foreign to you. You may think that someone is making a mountain out of a molehill, but when it comes to race, actual mountains are indeed made of countless molehills stacked on top of each other. Each one adds to the enormity of the problem of racism.

- **Nobody owes you a debate.** It is very hard on people of color to call out racism. Sometimes, that is the most they can do. And while you may really want to get it all sorted out right then and there, understand that when you ask to "talk it out" you are asking for more emotional labor from somebody who is already hurt. It is nice if you get it, and you should be grateful, but it is not owed you. You can still give this serious thought. You can still look deep inside yourself, you can still Google for more insight (remember, it's highly unlikely that anything you've done has not been done before), even if the person who brought this to your attention does not want to engage further.

- **Nobody owes you a relationship.** Even if you've recognized where you've been racist, worked to make amends, and learned from your mistakes, the person that you harmed does not owe you a relationship of any kind. In a hostile world, people of color have the right to cut off contact with people who have harmed them. They do not have to stick around to see all the progress you've made.

- **Remember that you are not the only one hurt.** Yes, it hurts to know that somebody thinks you are being racist. But you were not the first one hurt here—it is the deep hurt of racism that forced this person to confront you. Do not make this about your pain at being called out.

- **If you can see where you have been racist, or if you can see where your actions have caused harm, apologize and mean it.** Think about how you can make amends if possible, and how you can avoid those same harmful actions in the future. If you cannot see where you have been racist, take some more time to seriously consider the issue some more before declaring your actions "not racist." There have been conversations I've had about race with white people that ended in absolute denials, only to have that white person come back to me months later to say that they finally realized that their actions were racist and they were sorry for the harm they had caused, not only by their actions, but by their vigorous denial of my experiences.

- **If, after a lot of careful thought, you still do not see your actions as racist and feel strongly that this is simply a misunderstanding, do not then invalidate that person's hurt.** A true misunderstanding isn't so just because your intentions were not racist. A true misunderstanding is when your actions do not actually have a racist impact even though somebody thinks they might. If I hit you but do not intend to hit you, that is not a misunderstanding about whether or not I hit you. The situation you are in may be a misunderstanding—it does happen, even if it happens less often than you think. But even if it is, the pain of the person confronting you is real. Do not deny that. Do not call it silly. Explain your viewpoint if you feel it's necessary, and hope that explanation sheds light that helps that person see the situation the same way that you do, but don't deny someone's lived experience. Your goal is to find out if you are being racist, not to prove that you aren't, and to resolve a painful situation if possible.

This is not an easy process, and it is not at all fun. And at times, it seems never-ending. At times it may seem like no matter what you do, you are doing something wrong. But you have to try to adjust to the feelings of shame and pain that come from being confronted with your own racism. You have to get over the fear of facing the worst in yourself. You should instead fear unexamined racism. Fear the thought that right now, you could be contributing to the oppression of others and you don't know it. But do not fear those who bring that oppression to light. Do not fear the opportunity to do better.

seventeen

Talking is great, but what else can I do?

"I'M SURE IF WE COULD JUST TALK ABOUT IT, YOU'D have me all straightened out."

This was the stubborn insistence from a theater director who had just finished loudly repeating "nigger" to a group of people of color at what had at first been a wonderful dinner discussing an upcoming art project and how we could ensure that it would be inclusive. A lot of painstaking effort had gone into making sure that the people of color (many queer and trans) felt safe in this environment. It is very hard as a person of color to feel comfortable in Seattle, especially in the upper echelons of the local art scene. But we were bringing a different show to this theater, one that focused on voices of color and hoped to bring in a community of color.

So we had gathered for dinner to talk about how we could accomplish this.

Everything had been going well, until one of the theater directors, a white man, decided after what was likely a few too many drinks to tell a story that he felt required him to say "nigger" loudly and repeatedly, without warning. Each time he said it, people of color at the table flinched as the word hit. It wasn't just the word "nigger"—we've all heard it. It was the fact that it had come after we'd let our guard down, after so much effort to let us know we were safe.

The dinner ended very quickly after that.

Once it was over, the head of the group that was going to be performing let the director know that what had just gone down was unacceptable and that they would not feel comfortable performing unless the staff of the theater underwent racial justice and awareness training to ensure that this would not happen again.

The director looked at me pleadingly. He didn't need training. He knew a lot of black people. He grew up with black people. He was practically black himself. He just needed to talk. With me. He repeatedly insisted that if I could just sit with him in a bar and talk this out with him, whatever had caused him to drunkenly repeat "nigger" at a dinner table surrounded by people of color would never happen again.

But I did not want to talk with this man, especially not over drinks. I had just been talking with this man, we all had. We had just spent hours talking about racial and social justice, and he still decided to say "nigger." I wanted this man to take some action for change.

IF YOU WANT TO TALK ABOUT RACE, THERE IS PLENTY OF opportunity. There are countless memes you post, tons of outrage you can share, limitless "thought exercises" you can participate in. But it is easy to get caught up in this talk and think you are doing so much more than just that—talk.

While many people are afraid to talk about race, just as many use talk to hide from what they really fear: action. The more that I write about race, the more I've been surrounded by this talk disguised as action. From the white men using my Facebook and Twitter feeds as their own virtue signaling play-ground, to the white women sending me five-paragraph-long emails letting me know how the racial oppression of people of color makes them feel personally—I've seen how addicted people can get to the satisfaction of knowing they are say-ing all the right things, that they are having "deep conversa-tions"—so addicted that it becomes the end-all and be-all of their racial justice goals.

I write about concepts that I think people are not under-standing. I write about pieces of the puzzle that I think peo-ple aren't seeing. I write from perspectives that I think many people don't get to hear. I do not do this just to increase general knowledge. I do not do this just to make people feel better. I do this in the hopes that what I write and say, and what others write and say, will inform and inspire action.

But so often, that is missed.

Recently I was explaining online and on a local radio station why I will not be participating in a local protest march focusing on women's issues. I had been asked to speak, and told how very important it was that the event have speakers who were women of color, especially in a predominantly white area like Seattle. I asked what the commission for speaking was, and was told that speakers were expected to donate their time and services. I declined the invitation.

When I wrote about why I would not be participating in the march, I explained that I could not ignore how much the economic exploitation of women of color had contributed to the racial oppression of women of color. And I did not believe that women of color should be asked to put forth the emotional and mental labor of discussing their racial oppression to a majority white audience for free, especially an event with a large budget like this one. I was very careful in my explanation of why I felt that this ask was problematic, and how important it is for us to not further exploitation and oppression within our movements.

It wasn't long before I got a message in response from a white woman I didn't know. She understood that I didn't want to work for free, but she didn't understand how asking for that work had been exploitative. Could I please take the time to explain to her further, personally (and, I'm assuming, for free), so she could understand?

She is not alone. Countless people read my work about racial justice and instead of taking action, want to shake that Etch A Sketch like it never happened and ask for the same conversation all over again.

I've lost count of the times I've had to end a conversation with someone about race, because instead of listening and engaging they were trying to deny my experiences as a woman of color and bully me into agreeing with them, only to have them reach out later that day to ask me to join them for coffee in order to "talk some more" about the subject. After a few times of agreeing to "talk some more" and once again finding myself "talked over" I realized that "talk" was all they wanted to get out of it.

At least once a week an organization will ask me to come talk, free of charge, to them about race. They are big fans of my work and just want to be able to have their own private conversations with me. "We would like a safe space to really get educated," one said. These are people who have read my work, had likely stopped by on social media to "like" posts and leave encouraging comments. These are people who have read my words on the mental, physical, and financial exploitation of black people and especially black women and the way in which it contributes to oppression. They have read the pain in my stories, and it resonated with them enough that they wanted me to repeat it all on demand, for free. This is talk that will make them sad, make them frustrated, make them cry. But it won't make them take action. They want to feel better, but they don't want to *do* better.

Words matter, and I'm not just saying that because they are my job. Words help us interpret our world, and can be used to change the way in which we think and act. Words are always at the heart of all our problems, and the beginning of all our solutions.

We cannot understand race and racial oppression if we cannot talk about it. And we can never stop the racial oppression affecting millions of lives in this country if we do not understand how and why it has been able to hold such power over us for hundreds of years.

But understanding, on its own, will never equal action. There are a lot of complex issues out there that many of us have talked a lot about and understand fairly well. Take, for example, global warming. The vast majority of Americans believe in global warming and understand that it is likely brought on by pollution. And while we talk about global warming and worry about global warming, most of us go about our days the same as we did before we ever heard the term because it's just easier to talk than to do. And global warming continues.

Until we have dismantled the system of White Supremacy and racial oppression, we will always need to talk about it. And I hope that you will use what you've read in this book to talk about it more successfully. And I hope that, as you continue to have these conversations about race, you will see opportunities for action and use what you've learned from your conversations to make that action more effective at dismantling oppression.

Talk. Please talk and talk and talk some more. But also act. Act now, because people are dying now in this unjust system. How many lives have been ground up by racial prejudice and hate? How many opportunities have we already lost? Act and talk and learn and fuck up and learn some more and act again and do better. We have to do this all at once. We have to learn and fight at the same time. Because people have been waiting far too long for their chance to live as equals in this society.

IT IS EASY TO THINK THAT THE PROBLEM OF RACIAL OP-pression in this country is just too big. How on earth can we be expected to dismantle a complex system that has been functioning for over four hundred years? My answer is: piece by piece. If you are looking for some small steps you can take right now to help create real change in the fight against racial oppression, if you are looking for your little piece of the system you can dismantle, here are some ideas:

- **Vote local.** Your vote will never have more power than in local elections. This is where politicians and city and state officials have to work for your vote. And so often, this opportunity to flex local power is flushed away by those who only vote in big, sexy, national elections. Vote local and demand that anybody asking for your vote (from school board to city council to state senator) make racial justice a top priority.
- **Get in schools.** Do you know what the racial achievement gap is in your school district? Find out, and then ask your school board, principals, and teachers what they are doing to address it. Are your schools erasing the history and accomplishments of people of color from your child's textbooks? Are your children only learning about people of color in February? Let them know that an inclusive education that meets the needs of *all* students is a top priority for you, even if your child is not a child of color.
- **Bear witness.** If you are a white person and you see a person of color being stopped by police, if you see a person of color being harassed in a store: bear witness and offer to help, when it is safe to do so. Sometimes just the watchful presence of another white person will make others stop and consider their actions more carefully.
- **Speak up in your unions.** I've watched with pride these last few years as my mother has leveraged her privilege

at her union to help make her workplace more inclusive. A longtime union representative, my mom has not let a single meeting go by without asking about the union's goals to promote diversity and inclusivity. When her union wrote racial justice goals into their platform for the year, she called me beaming with pride. Unions have a lot of power to combat racial discrimination and disenfranchisement at work, but only if the union decides to make it a priority.

- **Support POC-owned business.** Economic exploitation is one of the cornerstones of racial oppression. You can help preserve financial independence for people of color by working with and spending your money with POC businesses.

- **Boycott banks that prey on people of color.** The recent housing crash brought many of the racist practices of some of our biggest banks to light, but banks have been exploiting and abusing people of color for hundreds of years. Banks that sell bad loans to people of color should not get your business. Banks that hike up interest rates for people of color should not get your business. Banks that discriminate against people of color should not get your business. If you make these despicable actions by banks too costly, they will stop doing them, but not before then.

- **Give money to organizations working to fight racial oppression and support communities of color.** There are groups out there fighting every day for people of color. They are running after-school programs, giving legal advice, providing job training, providing medical services, fighting school discrimination, and so much more. And this all costs money. Give what you can to groups like the ACLU, SPLC, Planned Parenthood, NAACP, National Immigrant Justice Center, National Council of La Raza, Native American Rights Fund, Native American Disability Law Center, Asian Americans Advancing Justice, and more. Reach out to people in your local community to see what local organizations could use your financial support.

- **Boycott businesses that exploit workers of color.** Many businesses rely on cheap labor from people of color working in unhealthy conditions. Boycott businesses that cut costs by cutting out respect and living wages for workers of color.

- **Support music, film, television, art, and books created by people of color.** So much of our cultural representation is white by default. Normalize the work of people of color by financially supporting it and asking your producers, museum owners, studios, radio stations, and publishers for more.

- **Support increases in the minimum wage.** Yes, there are many reasons why so many people of color are so much poorer than white people. But we cannot ignore the fact that a larger proportion of people of color work in lower-wage jobs, and that a raise in those wages will disproportionately help people of color and can help address the vast racial wealth gap in this country.

- **Push your mayor and city council for police reform.** It is almost guaranteed that whatever city or town you live in, its police force can better serve its population of color. Ask your mayor what he or she is doing to address racial bias in policing. What training are officers undergoing? Do your officers have body cams? What sort of civilian oversight is there when there has been a complaint of bias, discrimination, or abuse? Put pressure on your city government to make this a priority, and keep that pressure up, otherwise police unions will bully city government into supporting the status quo, even if it risks the lives of black and brown people in your neighborhood.

- **Demand college diversity.** If you are in college, getting ready for college, or have a kid going to college, let your college know that the diversity and inclusiveness of students, curriculum, *and* staff is a top priority for you. Make sure colleges know that you expect any quality higher-education institution to embrace and promote diversity if they expect your tuition money.
- **Vote for diverse government representatives.** Help put people of color into the positions of power where they can self-advocate for the change that their communities need. Support candidates of color and support platforms that make diversity, inclusion, and racial justice a priority.

I know that the issue of racism and racial oppression seems huge—and it is huge. But it is not insurmountable. When we look at it in its entirety, it seems like too much, but understand that the system is invested in you seeing it that way. The truth is, we all pull levers of this white supremacist system, every day. The way we vote, where we spend our money, what we do and do not call out—these are all pieces of the system. We cannot talk our way out of a racially oppressive system. We can talk our way into understanding, and we can then use that understanding to act.

I'll never forget the outrage in 2016 over a district prosecutor who refused to press charges against a cop who was filmed shooting an unarmed black man. People were tweeting their anger at the prosecutor, sharing Facebook posts about how frustrated they were that once again, a cop was going to get away with murder. But when I looked up information for the district attorney, I realized that he was up for reelection later that year. I immediately started replying to the Tweets and messages of frustration that I was seeing: "THIS PERSON IS RUNNING FOR REELECTION—GIVE YOUR MONEY TO HIS CHALLENGER. MAKE AN EXAMPLE OF HIM." Because I already knew that if moral arguments and outrage were going to persuade a district attorney to press charges against an officer for shooting an unarmed black person, we would have seen more than only eighteen officers charged with unlawful death in 2015, in over 1,100 killings of civilians by police that year. But everyone responds to threats to their livelihood. And declining to indict an officer when there is video proof of severe misconduct should be a decision that a prosecuting attorney cannot afford to make.

We saw that action take hold in the March 2015 reelection bid of Cook County State's Attorney Anita Alvarez, who after numerous high-profile police brutality cases where Alvarez was seen as less than responsive—including what many view to be a cover-up and thirteen-month delay in pressing charges in the horrific shooting of seventeen-year-old Laquan McDonald, who was shot sixteen times as he walked away from officers—was handed a resounding defeat to challenger

Kim Foxx. This defeat was the result not only of numerous protests in and around Chicago, but of organized efforts of Chicago activists to support Alvarez's challenger and get out the vote on election day. Not only was a prosecutor that many felt was a defender of police brutality and corruption removed from office, but a warning message was sent to prosecutors around the country: you cannot afford to protect a corrupt and violent police system.

You don't always win the fight at first, but small actions add up, especially when you don't give up. In my hometown of Seattle in 2016, activists were engaged in a fight with the city over plans to build the most expensive new police precinct in the country. In a city with a housing crisis leading to rising homelessness, school funding so poor that the state supreme court has declared that it is in violation of the state constitution, and a rising opioid addiction problem—many balked at the thought of spending $160 million on a new police building. Add to that the fact that the Seattle Police Department was found by the federal government in 2011 to be practicing widespread abuse against its citizens and put under consent decree to reform its practices, and the fact that the consent decree process still had not been completed as of 2016, many felt that our cops who had been dragging their feet at reform did not deserve a shiny new building with taxpayer dollars.

Yes, we talked about it on social media—spreading the word about why the prevention of this new department headquarters (nicknamed "the bunker") was important. But we also took action. City council meetings were filled with concerned citizens waiting hours for the public comment period to voice their shock that the city would be taking money that could go to so many in need, and giving it to a police system already found to be broken and failing in their promises of reform. At first, it was defeat after defeat. I remember taking my sons with me to a city council meeting where there were so many "Block the Bunker" people there that we were moved into an overflow room. We watched people get up to speak, sixty seconds each, for over two hours, only to have the City Council vote 11 to 1 to move forward with the project. My nine-year-old held his "Black Lives Matter" sign and asked "Why aren't they listening to us?"

But we didn't give up. The bunker was brought up at every public event the mayor or members of the city council attended. Every city council meeting, members of the council had to stare at an ocean of Seattleites wearing "Block the Bunker" T-shirts and holding "Black Lives Matter" signs. When the mayor voiced his intention to attend a highly popular community block party, he was informed by organizers that he could come, but they wanted him to know that they did not approve of his support of the new police headquarters. People wrote to our local newspapers and television stations asking them to increase their coverage of the Block the Bunker movement.

Eventually, the tide began to change. Our major local papers, usually the voice of the status quo, came out against the new headquarters. More city council members voiced their concern. Finally, after almost a year of protest, the mayor announced that he was shelving the $160 million project. Then activists, partnered with Seattle City Council member Kshama Sawant, were able to get the city to commit a large portion of those funds to low-income housing. It was one of the high-lights of my year to be able to tell my kids that they had helped bring positive change to our city, that we can accomplish just about anything if we don't give up.

All around the country people are effecting real change with small actions. Change that improves the lives of people of color in their towns and cities and weakens an oppressive system. Racial oppression starts in our homes, our offices, our cities, and our states, and it can end there as well. So start talking, not just problems, but solutions. We can do this, together.

Acknowledgments

THERE ARE SO MANY PEOPLE TO THANK. I HAVE BEEN so lucky in my life, I could fill an entire book with the names of those who have helped get me here. It is very stressful to boil down these acknowledgments to a page (or two), but I must try.

My mother, Susan, raised my brother and sister and me on her own, through extreme poverty and heartbreak. With all of the pressures that she was under, all of the ups and downs of being a single parent, not once in my life did I ever feel like she didn't love me. Not once in my life did I ever feel like she didn't believe in me, or that I had let her down. I realize now what a rare gift that is that she gave us. Mommy: Thank you. I love you. And I will change your diapers when you get old, I promise.

Acknowledgments

To my siblings, Ahamefule, Jacque, and Basil. Aham: You have been my closest companion throughout my entire life. When we were little and we were the only brown kids in school and we had no friends but each other, I remember standing with you in front of the bathroom mirror pointing out the things we liked about ourselves—the nose that people said was too wide, our brown eyes, our dark skin. You were my other "other." Thank you for being an annoying little bro for as long as I can remember. Jacque: I'm so proud of you and the woman you are becoming. You are an amazing aunt, a great sister, and a great friend. I'm excited to watch you charge down your own path in life. Basil: Thank you for being so persistent. Thank you for never giving up on the family that you knew was yours. You make our family stronger, and funnier. I'm so glad you're here.

Shane Kalles: Thank you for being the friend who visits in the hospital, the friend who has wished me a Happy Mother's Day every year for sixteen years, the friend who wrote me into his wedding vows, the friend who has known me since I was a mopey seventeen-year-old and has loved me every step of the way. I am not good at keeping friends, so thanks for keeping me. Joseph Becker: From the age of fifteen you were the best and the worst, the most infuriating and the funniest, and always the most stalwart friend in my life. Seeing how hard you fought for yourself encouraged me to go back to school. I never told you that, and you deserved the chance to lord that over me while you were here. I miss you, and I wish you could know that you are in this book, you asshole.

I had a sixth-grade teacher who used to keep me in at recess to redo classwork that she was sure was not my absolute best. She was convinced I could be a great writer one day, if only I would give it my all. For a long time as an adult, I forgot how much I had loved writing and spent many years ignoring the words that were inside me. But I never forgot that, on my last day of sixth grade, my teacher told me to dedicate my first book to her. So, Mrs. Fitzpatrick, wherever you are—you encouraging and infuriating taskmaster—this is for you.

This book would not exist without the work of strong black women both past and present who have changed the way we all think about black womanhood and have made the world better for it. Audre Lorde, Michelle Alexander, bell hooks, Kimberlé Crenshaw, Angela Davis, Toni Morrison, Alice Walker, Maya Angelou, and so many more amazing women. Thank you for the generosity of your intellect and spirit. I hope one day to enlighten, encourage, and inspire a fraction of as many young black women as you have done and continue to do.

This is a very hard business for black women to get into, let alone make a living off of. When I was just starting out, and scared to put my words out into the world, there were some amazingly kind and generous writers and editors who gave me council, encouragement, and opportunity. Thank you to Lindy West, Jess Zimmerman, Jennifer Cumby, Charles Mudede, and the entire crew at The Establishment: Nikki, Kelley, Katie, Jessica, and Ruchika.

And of course, this book would not exist if not for the enthusiasm of Seal Press, the watchful eye of my editor Laura Mazer, and the foresight and support of my agent Lauren Abramo—who knew I should write a book before I did and has promoted my work with zeal and care. Thank you Lauren for believing in me so strongly.

Some people are fortunate enough to have a light that guides their way through life. I have, since the age of twenty, been lucky enough to have been guided by the light of my insightful, kind, and creative son Malcolm and, since the age of twenty-six, his hilarious, curious, and compassionate brother Marcus as well. Malcolm and Marcus: everything good I've done in my adult life I've been able to do because you make me believe in the beautiful possibility of humankind. I will work the rest of my life to repay the gift that was given me when you came into this world. Thank you for blessing me with your love and wit. You have been my home for the last sixteen years, and I cannot imagine who I would be without you. I am so unbelievably proud of you both. You are magic, you are entire universes, you are the reason why.

Notes

chapter six: Is police brutality really about race?

1. Kim Soffen, "The Big Question About Why Police Pull Over So Many Black Drivers," *Washington Post*, July 8, 2016, https://www.washingtonpost.com/news/wonk/wp/2016/07/08/the-big-question-about-why-police-pull-over-so-many-black-drivers/.

2. Ibid.

3. David Montgomery, "Data Dive: Racial Disparities in Minnesota Traffic Stops," July 8, 2016, http://www.twincities.com/2016/07/08/data-dive-racial-disparities-in-minnesota-traffic-stops/; Sarah Ryley, "Minorities Face Disproportionate 'Broken Windows' Enforcement Everywhere—Especially in Predominately White Neighborhoods," September 8, 2014, http://www.nydailynews.com/new-york/nyc-crime/broken-windows-disproportionately-enforced-white-neighborhoods-article-1.1931171; Tyler Tynes, "Black People Ticketed for Not

Wearing Seat Belts in Florida Twice As Often As Whites," January 27, 2016, http://www.huffingtonpost.com/entry/florida-seat-belt-law-racial-disparity_us_56a8f6efe4b0f71799289fb1; Andrew Garber, "Seattle Blacks Twice As Likely to Get Tickets," June 14, 2000, http://community.seattletimes.nwsource.com/archive/?date=20000614&slug=4026674; Matthew Kauffman, "Blacks, Hispanics More Likely to Be Ticketed After Traffic Stops," May 10, 2015, http://www.courant.com/news/connecticut/hc-racial-profiling-ticket-no-ticket-p-20150510-story.html.

4. The Sentencing Project, "Report of The Sentencing Project Regarding Racial Disparities in the United States Criminal Justice System," *The Sentencing Project*, August 2015, http://sentencingproject.org/wp-content/uploads/2015/12/Race-and-Justice-Shadow-Report-ICCPR.pdf.

5. Tom Jackman, "Oakland Police, Stopping and Handcuffing Disproportionate Numbers of Blacks, Work to Restore Trust," *Washington Post*, June 15, 2016, https://www.washingtonpost.com/news/true-crime/wp/2016/06/15/oakland-police-stopping-and-handcuffing-disproportionate-numbers-of-blacks-work-to-restore-trust/.

6. Phillip Atiba Goff, Tracy Lloyd, Amanda Geller, Stephen Raphael, and Jack Glaser, "The Science of Justice: Race, Arrests, and Police Use of Force," *Policing Equity*, July 2016, http://policingequity.org/wp-content/uploads/2016/07/CPE_SoJ_Race-Arrests-UoF_2016-07-08-1130.pdf.

7. Frank Newport, "Public Opinion Context: Americans, Race and Police," July 8, 2016, http://www.gallup.com/opinion/polling-matters/193586/public-opinion-context-americans-race-police.aspx.

8. Victor E. Kappeler, "A Brief History of Slavery and the Origins of American Policing," January 7, 2014, http://plsonline.eku.edu/insidelook/brief-history-slavery-and-origins-american-policing.

9. Louisiana Department of Culture, Recreation and Tourism, "Louisiana State Museum Online Exhibits the Cabildo: Two Centuries of Louisiana History. Reconstruction I: A State Divided," n.d., http://

www.crt.state.la.us/louisiana-state-museum/online-exhibits/the
-cabildo/reconstruction-a-state-divided/.

10. Tanzina Vega, "Why the Racial Wealth Gap Won't Go Away," January 26, 2016, http://money.cnn.com/2016/01/25/news /economy/racial-wealth-gap/.

11. Meizhu Lui, "Doubly Divided: The Racial Wealth Gap," *Racial Equity Tools*, n.d., http://www.racialequitytools.org/resourcefiles /lui.pdf.

chapter seven: How can I talk about affirmative action?

1. The Leadership Conference, "Civil Rights 101: Affirmative Action," n.d., http://www.civilrights.org/resources/civilrights101/affirmaction .html.

2. Eilcen Patten, "Racial, Gender Wage Gaps Persist in U.S. Despite Some Progress," July 1, 2016, http://www.pewresearch.org /fact-tank/2016/07/01/racial-gender-wage-gaps-persist-in-u-s -despite-some-progress/.

3. Daniel Losen, Cheri Hodson, Michael A. Keith II, Katrina Morrison, and Shakti Belway, "Are We Closing the School Discipline Gap?" *The Civil Rights Project*, 2015, https://www.civilrightsproject .ucla.edu/resources/projects/center-for-civil-rights-remedies/school -to-prison-folder/federal-reports/are-we closing-the-school-discipline -gap/losen-are-we-closing-discipline-gap-2015-summary.pdf.

4. Walter S. Gilliam, Angela N. Maupin, Chin R. Reyes, Maria Accavitti, and Frederick Shic, "Do Early Educators' Implicit Biases Regarding Sex and Race Relate to Behavior Expectations and Recommendations of Preschool Expulsions and Suspensions?," *Yale Child Study Center*, September 28, 2016, http://ziglercenter.yale.edu /publications/Preschool%20Implicit%20Bias%20Policy%20Brief_final _9_26_276766_5379.pdf.

5. Hua-Yu Cherng, "Is All Classroom Conduct Equal?: Teacher Contact with Parents of Racial/Ethnic Minority and Immigrant Adolescents," *Teachers College Record*, 2016, http://www.tcrecord.org /Content.asp?ContentId=21625.

6. Grant H. Blume and Mark C. Long, "Changes in Levels of Affirmative Action in College Admissions in Response to Statewide Bans and Judicial Rulings," June 2014, http://journals.sagepub.com/doi /pdf/10.3102/0162373713508810.

7. Hayley Munguia, "Here's What Happens When You Ban Affirmative Action in College Admissions," December 9, 2015, https:// fivethirtyeight.com/features/heres-what-happens-when-you-ban -affirmative-action-in-college-admissions/.

chapter eight: What is the school-to-prison pipeline?

1. Carla Amurao, "Fact Sheet: How Bad Is the School-to-Prison Pipeline?," 2013, http://www.pbs.org/wnet/tavissmiley/tsr/education -under-arrest/school-to-prison-pipeline-fact-sheet/; Libby Nelson and Dara Lind, "The School to Prison Pipeline, Explained," February 24, 2015, http://www.justicepolicy.org/news/8775.

2. A National Summit on Zero Tolerance, "Opportunities Suspended: The Devastating Consequences of Zero Tolerance and School Discipline," *The Civil Rights Project*, June 2000, https://www .civilrightsproject.ucla.edu/research/k-12-education/school -discipline/opportunities-suspended-the-devastating-consequences -of-zero-tolerance-and-school-discipline-policies/crp-opportunities -suspended-zero-tolerance-2000.pdf.

3. Nelson and Lind, "The School to Prison Pipeline, Explained."

4. Ibid.

5. Ibid.

6. Julianne Hing, "Race, Disability and the School-to-Prison Pipeline," May 13, 2014, http://www.colorlines.com/articles/race -disability-and-school-prison-pipeline.

7. Nelson and Lind, "The School to Prison Pipeline, Explained."

chapter twelve: What are microaggressions?

1. Kevin L. Nadal, Katie E. Griffin, Yinglee Wong, Sahran Hamit, and Morgan Rasmus, "The Impact of Racial Microaggressions on Mental Health: Counseling Implications for Clients of Color," *Wiley Online Library*, January 7, 2014, http://onlinelibrary.wiley.com/doi

/10.1002/j.1556-6676.2014.00130.x/abstract?systemMessage=WOL
+Usage+report+download+page+will+be+unavailable+on+Friday
+27th+January+2017+at+23%3A00+GMT%2F+18%3A00+EST
%2F+07%3A00+SGT+%28Saturday+28th+Jan+for+SGT%29++for
+up+.

chapter fourteen: What is the model minority myth

1. Huizhong Wu, "The 'Model Minority' Myth: Why Asian-American Poverty Goes Unseen," December 14, 2015, http://mashable.com/2015/12/14/asian-american-poverty/#.UK4LnHskgqr.

2. "Students Reject the 'Model Minority Myth,'" October 15, 2014, http://college.usatoday.com/2014/10/15/students-reject-the-model-minority-myth/.

3. Guofang Li, "Other People's Success: Impact of the 'Model Minority' Myth on Underachieving Asian Students in North America," 2005, https://msu.edu/~liguo/file/KEDI%20Journal-Guofang%20Li%202005%5B1%5D.pdf.

4. Sahra Vang Nguyen, "The Truth About 'The Asian Advantage' and 'Model Minority Myth,'" October 14, 2015, http://www.huffingtonpost.com/sahra-vang-nguyen/the-truth-about-the-asian_b_8282830.html.

5. US Census Bureau, "Educational Attainment of the Population Aged 25 and Older by Age, Sex, Race and Hispanic Origin, and Other Selected Characteristics," March 2016, http://www.census.gov/content/dam/Census/library/publications/2016/demo/p20-578.pdf.

6. Julie Siebens and Camille L. Ryan, "Field of Bachelor's Degree in the United States: 2009," *United States Census Bureau*, February 2012, https://www.census.gov/prod/2012pubs/acs-18.pdf.

7. Liza Mundy, "Cracking the Bamboo Ceiling," November 2014, http://www.theatlantic.com/magazine/archive/2014/11/cracking-the-bamboo-ceiling/380800/.

8. Jeff Yang, "Tech Industry Needs This Secret Weapon," August 27, 2014, http://www.cnn.com/2014/08/27/opinion/yang-tech-diversity/.

9. The Sikh Coalition, "Fact Sheet on Post-9/11 Discrimination and Violence Against Sikh Americans," *The Sikh Coalition*, n.d., http://www.sikhcoalition.org/images/documents/fact%20sheet%20on%20hate%20against%20sikhs%20in%20america%20post%209-11%201.pdf.

10. Amy Van Arsdale, "Asian/Pacific Islander Domestic Violence Resource Project," *DVRP*, June 2014, http://dvrp.org/wp-content/uploads/2014/06/Project-AWARE-Fact-Sheet.pdf.

chapter sixteen: I just got called racist, what do I do now?

1. Ken Tucker, "George Bush Really Does Not 'Appreciate' Kanye West's Katrina Criticism: 'The Worst Moment of My Presidency,'" November 2, 2010, http://www.ew.com/article/2010/11/02/george-bush-kanye-west-lauer-today.